Choices

Finding God's Way in Dating, Sex,
Singleness, and Marriage

STACY & PAULA
RINEHART

NAVPRESS
BRINGING TRUTH TO LIFE
P.O. Box 35001, Colorado Springs, Colorado 80935

OUR GUARANTEE TO YOU

We believe so strongly in the message of our books that we are making this quality guarantee to you. If for any reason you are disappointed with the content of this book, return the title page to us with your name and address and we will refund to you the list price of the book. To help us serve you better, please briefly describe why you were disappointed. Mail your refund request to: NavPress, P.O. Box 35002, Colorado Springs, CO 80935.

The Navigators is an international Christian organization. Our mission is to reach, disciple, and equip people to know Christ and to make Him known through successive generations. We envision multitudes of diverse people in the United States and every other nation who have a passionate love for Christ, live a lifestyle of sharing Christ's love, and multiply spiritual laborers among those without Christ.

NavPress is the publishing ministry of The Navigators. NavPress publications help believers learn biblical truth and apply what they learn to their lives and ministries. Our mission is to stimulate spiritual formation among our readers.

FOR A FREE CATALOG OF
NAVPRESS BOOKS & BIBLE STUDIES.
CALL 1-800-366-7788 (USA)
or 1-416-499-4615 (CANADA)

Contents

ᘒ ᘔ ᘒ

To
Gordon and Brenda Van Amburgh
and
John and Karen D'Arrezo
whose help and influence
guided the choices we made
concerning dating, courtship, and marriage

Acknowledgments

ↄ ↄ ⌒

This book has grown out of years of relationships with fascinating people struggling to understand what it means to walk with God in this thing called "being single." We could not have written it the first time—or revised it now—without the help of many of those folks. To Brenda and Gordon Van Amburg and John and Karen D'Arrezzo we say thanks for putting us on track ourselves, many years ago, and helping us discover what it meant to trust God in this area of our lives. To a host of students at Oklahoma State University and singles in Tulsa, Oklahoma we owe a special debt for what they taught us through their relationships. And we are also grateful to a group of singles at the Church of the Holy Cross in Raleigh—especially Anisa, Kelly, Pete, Joel, and Mark—for the insight they've added about relationships, as they see them.

Preface

Ꙩ Ꙩ ꙭ

Paula, I give you this ring as a token of my love for you. God has built into you the qualities essential to become my wife. You've added joy, creativity, and beauty to my life. I promise to love you, constantly giving up my rights for you even as Christ did for His bride, the Church. I promise to lead you as God directs in our lives and to be responsible for your well-being and the well-being of our children. I always want you to be my best friend. Regardless of what happens in our lives, we can rejoice and enjoy life because God has enclosed us in His hand. We love, Paula, because God first loved us.

Ꙩ Ꙩ ꙭ

Stacy, because I have seen God lead us together in such a special way, I give myself to making our marriage and our life such that the world looking on will know that He is real. I promise that I will love you in the midst of the everydayness of life. I promise that I will live openly and honestly before you so that we would not live out our lives in separation and isolation. Because I trust you with my life, I promise that I will defer to your leadership. Before God and before men, you will be the head of our home. And so do not urge me to leave you or to turn back from following you. For where you go, I will go; where you lodge, I will lodge. Your people will be my people and your God, my God. And thus may the Lord do to me and worse, if anything but death should part you and me.

○ ○ ○

These are the words we began life together with on August 4, 1973. And what a journey it has been! Our children are half-grown, we've lived in a variety of interesting places, we've enjoyed some wonderful times—and weathered some tough ones—together through the years. It becomes clearer all the time how much impact our choices as singles have actually had on our lives together.

That's the vantage point from which we have written this book. *The choices you are making now—as a high school or college student, as an older single—really do matter.* We'd like to help you take the time to really think through those choices.

Perhaps you are wondering what a couple who has been married almost a quarter of a century now would venture to say to someone who is single. Believe it or not, by this point in our lives we have watched countless single people get together and get married. We have even played a part in some of those mergers! We know what it is to help someone with the particular loneliness of longing to share his or her life with another person—and that person just hasn't come along. We know what it means to make the transition from "doing relationships" like everyone around you . . . to allowing the authority and grace of Christ to invade even this terribly personal area of life.

But mostly we have written this book out of gratitude. We are deeply thankful for the years the Lord has given us together—and we are aware that the blessings of those years have grown out of the grace of having come to know the Lord as single people. That meant that we—like you—were afforded the special opportunity to ground our lives and our relationships in the principles that God gives. God made each of us a man or a woman for a reason and He knows what it takes to make a relationship work for a lifetime. Getting together was His idea from the start.

You may have picked up this book out of curiosity, wondering if the Bible has anything relevant to say to the world of relationships in which you find yourself. We want to assure you, it does! You may be reading at a time when the biggest thing you feel when you think of the opposite sex is burned. Perhaps you've been disappointed. Whatever brings you to this book—or however you may be feeling—we want to encourage you to read on. Our prayer is that you will find in these pages good reason to hope that the truth God offers us about relationships—dating, relating, and choosing a lifelong partner—are infinitely preferable to anything we could have dreamed up on our own.

Stacy and Paula Rinehart
August 1995

CHAPTER ONE

Going Against the Grain of Your Culture

ᦉ ᦉ ᦉ

Imagine yourself in a new restaurant reading a fancy menu on an empty stomach. You spend a few minutes deciphering the delicacies listed and then give your order. "I believe I'll try this roast duckling with chestnut sauce, please." When the plate arrives, you express your approval of a beautiful arrangement of food, complete with complementary colors and garnishes. "It's worth blowing a diet for food like this," you remark.

About halfway through the meal, you begin to have second thoughts. The chestnuts are lodging in your throat. It seems like that duck and your stomach are fighting over mineral rights. "Maybe my eyes are bigger than my stomach," you explain with a note of regret as you push back your plate. Mentally you resolve to ask a few questions and make a wise decision the next time you look at an unfamiliar menu.

Many people go through similar pangs of regret concerning their decisions about dating and marriage. Relationships that are appealing at the outset can turn distasteful with time. The gentle wound of Cupid's arrow can become a painful thorn in the flesh, and many who swear by their commitment to each other soon find that they are swearing at it. In fact, most current research claims that, statistically, each of us has about a fifty-fifty chance for a lasting and happy marital union. As one counselor said,

> There are many people living heaven on earth and they call it marriage and many people living hell on earth and they call it marriage. You can only rejoice with people who have discovered a partner and have been able to work out a relationship under divine principles and with divine enabling that is something close to heaven on earth. And you can only bleed for those people who for a variety of reasons are in a situation where they are living in a daily, constant hell.[1]

No relationship that joins two fallen human beings is perfect, to be sure—but what a difference the power of Christ can make in a marriage where both individuals belong to Him.

It's amazing to think about how little forethought most of us give to this, the most significant of all our human relationships. Somewhere in adolescence our hormones kick into gear and usually we just migrate mindlessly in some direction toward the opposite sex as though on automatic pilot. Years ago, the "parlor" functioned as a way to let younger men and women meet safely, always under the watchful eye of family. We sometimes look at cultures that still practice arranged marriages and think of them as a bit backward. The point, though, is that wise people in any culture recognize an important truth: good relationships— ones that last a lifetime—don't just happen by chance. It takes forethought on *someone's* part.

We're advocating that you use this book as your own

time to think—or rethink—the messages you've received about how men and women relate well. What makes a good match between two individuals? Where does God figure into the picture? What do you, as an individual, bring to it all? The Bible doesn't speak directly to cultural practices like "dating," but it sure offers a collection of unbeatable principles that operate almost like relational laws of gravity.

OUR STORY

Before we look more deeply at the messages our culture bombards us with, we'd like to tell you some of our story as single people. The question, of course, is what can a couple who met in the era of love beads and bell bottoms share with you that hits home? More than you might imagine, we think. As is so often true, the personal is universal. And there is nothing quite so universal as falling in love.

The first time I fell in love, I was sixteen—young, impressionable, and totally unaware of how much love could hurt. One evening, at a party with friends, I spotted this guy across the room and something in his face just plain intrigued me. I had to meet him. That was the beginning of a romance that lasted well into my college years. In spite of the fact that his deepest love was basketball, he somehow fit me into his life. He was quiet and intense and possessing but one flaw in my opinion: he was a minister's son. You can believe that we spent no small amount of time in church. Slowly, inexorably, almost against my will, I came face to face with the One who would become, in a much truer sense, my First Love (in the words of Revelation 2:4). Over a period of months, I listened to Paul's argument for Christianity in the book of Romans and, as they say, I encountered Christ.

I have to admit that I didn't really know what to do with

those two new relationships. On one hand, this guy and I were becoming more and more involved. We were nearly inseparable, beginning to plan our future as though we'd be together inside the same picture frame. But we also got on each other's nerves. Surely jealousy and selfishness weren't supposed to be this big of a problem in a relationship, I reasoned. And the physical stuff—as the months went by, that got out of control too. Free-floating guilt became an undertow, a weight in a relationship already sagging under too much strain.

But I had also grown well past the "introduction phase" in my relationship with Christ. More and more He seemed real to me, like Someone I could spend eternity really getting to know. It felt as though He was pulling me—away from this guy, away from everything known and familiar—to a future I could only guess at. I had to follow—it was as simple, and as difficult, as that. The psalmist claims that God will not withhold anything from us that He considers good for us (Psalm 84:11). And it was becoming painfully clear that we were not the "good thing" God had in mind for each other. For quite a while, the two of us hung in limbo—miserable with each other, miserable without each other. When we finally parted halfway through college it felt like a miniature divorce, but I knew it was the right thing to do. Getting out of his car for the last time and closing the door on that relationship ended a long chapter in my life.

Even in the painful aloneness of that ending, though, I was amazed at how the Lord began to step into my life, more real and exciting than I had ever imagined. In some strange way, He seemed enough. He was grounding me—as an individual, as a woman—like a small oak tree that is planted close to a stream so that its roots can sink deep.

Of course, this story begs the question of how Stacy and I met—since I obviously didn't marry the first guy I fell in love with. We met in a carpool, actually. Forty minutes each way to a summer job, I attempted the Herculean feat of trying to get (another) quiet, intense man to talk! After two weeks I was nearly ready to admit defeat. And then one day, the conversation turned to racquetball. It was just like someone had pulled Stacy's string. On and on he rambled about the racquetball tournaments he organized in the army and how he loved the sport. I listened in shock, my mouth slightly ajar. Then, even more unexpectedly, he began to turn the tables and ask me questions. Had I played much? How long was my racquet? How many sides to a court did I prefer? It embarrasses me to this day to admit this—but I completely made up the answers. My only defense is that I was willing to do anything to keep this remarkable conversation afloat.

As soon as I got out of the car, I was stabbed with the realization that I had lied. I would have to admit the truth— I had never played racquetball. I wouldn't know a racquetball from an Easter egg. My confession of the truth, though, somehow broke the ice and we spent the rest of the summer getting to know each other. I guess Stacy felt, and he was right—any woman that desperate deserved better company.

Stacy and I had a particular advantage that summer. We were part of a Christian program for singles and college students in which everyone voluntarily agreed to suspend the practice of going out as couples. So we just talked . . . and talked and talked. It's amazing how much you learn about someone when you aren't punctuating the conversation with anything like a kiss or a hug, much less more. In a strange way, it was very freeing. I got to know Stacy's goals and dreams and his background. We went our separate ways at the end of the summer, relying primarily on tapes sent through the mail to continue the relationship. We were both wondering if, perhaps, God might be leading us together. All I could say was that I knew I had met a man I really *respected*.

We gave another six months to getting to know each other and spending a lot of time in prayer. It's hard to over-estimate the importance of prayer. I am convinced that God is the ultimate Matchmaker and He cares far more about finding the love of our lives than even we do. Deep into the month of March, Stacy felt he had the green light from the Lord. Marriage became his new goal. He wasted no time in that pursuit, calling me long distance late one night, from a pay phone outside a K-Mart in Texas to ask if I would marry him. It's hard to explain in words that make sense — but I *knew* that "yes" was the answer I was meant to give to that question. Yes, I would marry him.

Marry we did, in the hot month of August in Virginia, with pews full of family and friends. Then we did what we now advise couples never to do if they can help it. We packed all our earthly belongings in a One Way Ryder van and moved halfway across the country to a town in Texas where we knew no one. Stacy had one more year of college and four years of seminary to finish. Talk about two people having to pull together to make it work!

Now, twenty years later, a curious thing happens. Sin-gles, usually younger than we are, will occasionally make an amazing comment to this effect: "Well," they will say, "I just can't find a man or a woman who seems as solid or sensi-tive or committed or whatever quality (fill in the blank) I see in you two." Not that we are by any means finished prod-ucts — but the implication is that there are no more already-put-together specimens of men and women remaining. There are none left. I always wish I could roll back the years and introduce them to "us" when we met. What would they have seen? Two green, fairly naive individuals with some very rough and tattered edges who grew up together over one thousand cups of coffee and honest conversation. The best word that can be said after twenty years together is that God is very, very good.

THE MESSAGES FROM OUR CULTURE

We aren't, by any means, holding up our relationship as The Pattern to follow. But we hope you can see, in our story, the same threads of intrigue and romance, of pain and wonder that have woven the tapestry of dating—and mating— through every generation. Chances are, our story has many common elements to your own. The truth is that each of us must chart our own course through this territory of relationships between the sexes. And the only way we can do that is to take a hard, cold look at the messages we hear around us and compare those to the truth God has given us in His Word—truth that is given not to cramp our style, *but to provide us with something better.*

We are living in a time that is riddled with myths about how men and women, guys and girls should relate to each other. Jeremiah was one of those Old Testament prophets who blatantly warned the Israelites not to "learn the ways of the nations" around them, because their "customs were worthless" (Jeremiah 10:2-3). Translated into our vernacular, you and I need to look carefully at the path God has provided because the highway of the world will lead us nowhere we really want to go. What are the messages, "the customs," modern society bombards us with about relationships?

LIVING FOR THE MOMENT
When our daughter was learning to talk, she had trouble saying her last name, Rinehart. When asked her name, she often replied, "Allison Right Now!" Actually it was no wonder

she thought that was her last name because her daily chatter contained a barrage of "right now."

In "adult-speak" we call the demand to have what we want right now "instant gratification." We are led to believe that we can approach life and relationships with a vending machine mentality. You look over the possibilities, put your change in the slot, and pick out whatever suits your fancy. The philosophy of living for the moment is everywhere. "If it feels good, do it." Why should we have to wait—or experience pain—or live without our needs being met—now?

John and Pat were two young Christians who had known each other only a short time before they came to us for premarital counseling. They thought they loved each other—and in that first blush, thrilled-for-the-moment way maybe they did. But there was an awful lot of lust in their "love." They desperately needed to give the relationship *time*. And time was what they least wanted to endure. They married within the following few weeks.

When the initial attraction to each other wore off, they discovered they'd married someone they didn't really know. Five difficult years of financial woes, small children, and marital counseling testified to the repercussions of living for the pleasure of the moment. As we have watched and counseled them in some of the difficulties of those years, we only wished we had said *wait* a little louder.

Some ministers actually refuse to marry couples who have not known each other for at least six months. It simply takes time to let the facets of an individual's personality unfold.

Many people also hold the same kind of temporary, only-as-long-as-it's-pleasant mentality toward the very institution of marriage itself. From the shop that advertises "we rent wedding rings" to the idea of seeing marriage as a contract of convenience for "as long as our love lasts," we are wildly short on this notion of permanence.

It's not unusual to hear someone contemplating marriage or a newly married couple admit that they're going *to wait and see if their relationship works out* before they have children. Certainly, bringing children into a broken marriage is tragic — but it's equally mistaken to consider a relationship that's meant to be a lifelong union much the same way you'd buy a new car on trial to see if it really meets your needs.

Of course, marriage as God means for it to be holds significance far beyond two people moving into the same house with a signed marriage license. Marriage has a spiritual dimension. That's why it's such a travesty to treat it with an air of temporariness. Marriage is the symbolic picture of Christ's union with His bride, the Church (Ephesians 5:23). In spite of our unfaithfulness as the bride, He is committed to us for all eternity. Based on that relationship, marriage is for keeps. It doesn't even resemble the mentality of living for the moment. To people who live for the moment, the Christian's concept of lifelong commitment to one person stands out in sharp contrast.

Scripture uses a vocabulary quite different from our generation and modern society. In the Bible we see synonyms for words like *discipline, restraint, waiting, responsibility*, and *commitment*. Though it might sometimes appear that God would like to thwart all of our fun, nothing could be further from the truth. "For I know the plans I have for you. . . . They are plans for good and not for evil, to give you a future and a hope" (Jeremiah 29:11, TLB).

When I was a young but growing Christian, God began speaking to me about habits in my dating life that were hindering my spiritual growth. It was particularly hard to stop going out with men who, it was obvious to me, weren't Christians. That just wasn't their mindset — God didn't figure into

their plans. But I didn't know many guys who were Christians—and the ones who were often didn't go out! I knew if
I wasn't going out with nonChristians I would probably be
sitting home alone.

It took a lot of courage to narrow the field. One verse
I found—and still find—myself returning to was 1 Peter
2:6 (NASB): "He who believes in Him shall not be disappointed." I had some intuitive sense (which the Bible con-
firms) that charting a narrower course now would mean
more and better options in the future. That is really the
message of Jesus' teaching about choosing the narrow road
that leads to life.

We have to be able—and willing—to make choices in
the moment that seem hard because we know that, in the
long run, God has something good—very good—for us in
mind.

LIVING FOR THE SENSUAL

In the arena of sexuality, our generation (the Baby Boomers
born after World War II) is responsible for breaking all the
rules. Sex before marriage, sex with multiple partners, sex
as recreation—since the dawn of time there have always
been those who let sensuality determine their relationships.
The difference is that everyone knew that was wrong. Before
the '60s, such behavior was called immorality, pure and
simple. No one tried to excuse or justify those kinds of
choices. Our generation came along and arrogantly insisted
we could break all the rules—and not suffer the consequences. "Easy love," it was called.

What has happened? Add up AIDS and sexually trans-
mitted diseases, rising divorce, children born to unwed
mothers, and a trail of broken hearts and you tend to con-
clude that we were dead wrong. In Scriptural language, we
were kicking against goads. The harder you kick against

the boundary, the more pain you experience. God places enormous sexual freedom and joy within the limits of marriage, but He drew a fence around that relationship, for many reasons.

If we could take the attitude of modern society concerning sex, turn it upside down and inside out and discard some of it entirely, we might begin to approach the instructions that God gave in the first place. Just as a car manual gives detailed information as to the use and abuse of your car, so God has given us such clear directions about sex because our sexuality sits close to the core of our being. It colors so much of our lives — how we see ourselves as men and women, and how we treat others.

Consider the irony of it all. The same God who spoke the world into existence also masterminded our physical relationships, and yet the world acts as if He were some prudish old maid ready to give us a slap on the wrist for holding hands. God declared that all He had made was "very good" (Genesis 1:31). He devoted one book in the Bible, Song of Songs (Song of Solomon), primarily to a description of the heights of physical enjoyment possible in married love.

Many people have a shortsighted, painfully inadequate understanding of all that God meant sex to be. Sex involves all that you are as a person brought together with another whole person to reflect the complete oneness of Christ and His bride, the Church. Sex is special precisely because it's shared with only one person. One author as he surveyed the wounded, broken lives that flow from an attitude of sexual permissiveness, wisely said, "I have some theories and one of them is that one of the ways you measure love is not with words, but with actions, with commitment, with what you are willing to give up, with what you are willing to share with no one else."[2]

LIVING FOR SOMEONE WHO LOVES YOU

"You're Nobody Till Somebody Loves You" is the refrain of an old song. For much of our adolescent years and then some, we're subtly led to believe that when we find that special someone, our lives will take on real meaning. Our personalities will blossom, and our imperfections will disappear.

Many people wake up in married life to realize that what once seemed like moonlight and roses is now daylight and dishes. They are the same people with the same fears, old habits, and insecurities that they had before marriage. And they are each married to someone who will help point out these inconsistencies! Finding the love of your life is not the ultimate answer to your deep, personal needs.

Happiness is about having someone to love you, in a way—if the someone is really Someone. Augustine's famous metaphor is that we all have a vacuum inside us that only God can fill. Occasionally now you hear an expression used in addiction and recovery circles that each of us has a "hole in our souls." C. S. Lewis said that we bear, all our lives, an "inconsolable longing," an innate awareness of our incompleteness that is, ultimately, only resolved when we are present with the Lord.

What do most of us do with this sense of incompleteness, this inconsolable longing, this deep longing to be loved? We head off on a lifelong search for a person or a place or a thing who, as the illusion goes, can take away the emptiness. Especially we look for someone . . . someone who can keep our cup filled to the brim.

The search for someone is a powerful thing—it has to be, because so many things are sold on the back of that motivation. The right mouthwash will pave the way to the ultimate romance. A new, sleek car comes equipped with a beautiful woman in the front seat. Just pick up any copy of the personal ads to read as you munch a bagel to start the day. The message is that whatever happens, whatever you do, you must not be alone. You are no one until someone loves you. And so it goes.

When you buy into the myth—you're no one until there's someone in your life who loves you—you can end up holding onto a relationship far too long (just as I did). Or compromising convictions you hold dear. Or overlooking character flaws in another person that are obvious red lights on the dashboard of his or her life. All in the futile effort to avoid being *alone*, alone with yourself and God. For many of us, that's a fate worse than death. The strange part is that facing that aloneness isn't really so bad—if you can keep from letting "being alone" mean "being unwanted, unloved." The two are not the same. God *is* there, in the most painful places we run from. In His embrace we truly become ourselves; we become a "me" which is a necessity in order to ever be successfully connected to someone else as a "we."

Finding yourself as a person who has been and is being made complete in Christ, as the Apostle Paul said, is what it's all about (Colossians 2:10). Having your cup filled by Him is what lets you focus, in real and honest ways, on giving—rather than just getting—from a relationship. What makes a relationship between two Christians different is that it's not just between two people. There is a Third Party who is actively involved. Inside our wedding bands Paula and I had this verse inscribed: "We love because he first loved us" (1 John 4:19). It's His love that has to flow through a relationship—ours alone is never enough.

We can't deny that love is a wonderful thing. It can make you smile through the pouring rain. It comes well recommended. Love is a wonderful thing, but it's not *life*. The Bible says this so clearly, in so many ways. Paul claimed that it was as though the old you had died and your real life was hidden now in Christ (Colossians 3:3). John said that the summary of Jesus' death and resurrection is that God has given us life in Him. ". . . And this life is in his Son" (1 John 5:11).

The real truth is that life takes on meaning as our happiness comes from being loved, not by somebody—but by Somebody.

THE CHOICE BELONGS TO EACH OF US

When Stacy and I were first married, I had the same dream several times. I would be floating through a fog down the aisle of a church to marry a man whose face was sometimes indistinguishable and sometimes that of a former boyfriend. Always the same sick feeling in my stomach cautioned me that I was making a mistake. As I reached the end of the aisle, I would awaken in a cold sweat and then be flooded with relief that the person next to me was Stacy and that I had not made a mistake. I would lie there and thank God as I went back to sleep.

After marriage I could appreciate, much more fully, the significance of my earlier choices. Sometimes they were only small ones; often they were quite painful. But those choices made a big difference—in many cases they set a course for the whole direction of my life.

Choices are like that for all of us. The illusion of youth is, "I have all my life before me. My choices right now won't make any difference." Yet in the span of a few short but crucial years, decisions are made that open or close some doors for a lifetime. All of a sudden it's too late to develop solid friendships with the opposite sex, or exercise more sexual restraint, or study harder and party less. Life has moved on.

Going against the grain of your culture means a willingness to reject a sensual, self-centered lifestyle. The choices entailed are often complex and almost always require some backbone. Any time we yield an area of our lives to the Lord, we encounter a struggle. A woman who worked with college students once wrote, "Christianity isn't a narcotic that dulls you into obedience. It involves battle — it's excruciating to give up control. . . . Heaven will not be filled with innocent people, running around saying, 'Oh, was there another way? I guess I never noticed.'"[3]

The messages around us are loud and strong and relentless. It takes some spiritual guts to choose another path. It requires that our minds have to be transformed, just as Paul says in Romans 12:2, so that we think differently — and then act and choose differently.

Before we take a closer look at how that different approach may affect our choices before we marry, we need to look at the nature of the lifelong union we know as marriage.

Notes
1. Stuart Briscoe, from the tape "A Call to Singleness."
2. Richard Cohen, "Open Marriage . . . Broken Marriage," *The Washington Post*, as quoted by Charles R. Swindoll in *Strike the Original Match* (Portland, Oreg.: Multnomah, 1980), pp. 36-37.
3. Rebecca Pippert, *Out of the Saltshaker* (Downers Grove, Ill.: Inter-Varsity, 1979), p. 64.

Questions for Personal Study and Application

1. List the sources that have most influenced your dating patterns.
2. Describe a dating relationship in your past. How did culture influence this relationship? How did Scripture influence this relationship?
3. Read Genesis 25:29-34.
   a. How did Esau live for the moment, and what were the consequences?
   b. In what ways do you see Esau's attitude reflected in your decision making?
4. Read 2 Samuel 11:1–12:15.
   a. How did David live for the sensual?
   b. What were the consequences of his sin?
5. In what way, if any, have you been living for the sensual? What will you do to change this?
6. Read Genesis 39.
   a. What are some character qualities that prevented Joseph from taking advantage of his regular opportunity for sin with Potiphar's wife?
   b. What are some principles from Joseph's life that can be applied to dating?
7. Define idolatry in your own words. According to God's word in 1 Corinthians 5:11 and 10:14, and Ephesians 5:5, what is His perspective on idolatry in our lives?
8. Read Romans 12:1-2.
   a. What does it mean to present your bodies as a living and holy sacrifice, acceptable to God?
   b. Have you ever presented yourself as a living sacrifice to God? What about your dating life?
9. Jot down one or two significant applications that you will make from this study.

Suggested Scripture Memory

Romans 12:1

Questions for Discussion

Each group of questions below is for your use in discussing the corresponding questions on the previous page. Notice that, here and in the chapters that follow, discussion questions are not given for every personal study question (there are no discussion questions for questions 5 and 9). You may want to ask some of your own questions.

1. What do you think are some of the reasons why the divorce rate is so high in this culture? In what way do you think modern dating practices have a bearing on the high divorce rate?
2. The authors maintain that modern society contributes to our concept of dating. Do you agree? Why?
3. If you had been present when Jacob and Esau had this encounter, what would you have encouraged Esau to do, and why?
4. If you were a counselor of King David, how would you have counseled him when he first saw Bathsheba?
6. Scan the section on "Living for the Moment." In what ways do you feel this temptation? How does this philosophy affect your life? Read James 4:1-4. What are the results of living for pleasures and lusts (sensuality)? The Bible says that a pleasure-centered life is living like everyone else in the world lives. What are the results of being a friend of the world?
7. In what ways can a dating relationship become an idol? How can you tell if that is happening to you?
8. If a person has presented himself as a living sacrifice, what differences would it make in his relationships with the opposite sex?

CHAPTER TWO

Priceless Principles

○ ○ ○

Why would someone who's single devote much time and effort into thinking about the whole idea of marriage? Doesn't that seem like something way down the road — far removed from the party on Friday night or the attractive new girl an old friend introduced you to last week? Besides, suppose a person never gets married, anyway?

Actually, looking at the whole picture around the idea of marriage makes sense when you consider that most of us do end up, at some point in our lives, standing before the altar of a church exchanging vows — marriage vows. We have a friend who is in her late fifties — and she is getting married this fall, for the first time, to a wonderful widower she has known for years.

What few of us realize, as single people, is that we will carry an invisible suitcase into whatever relationship we choose for a lifetime. And in that suitcase will be a collection of all we've learned in relating to the opposite sex. The sum total of our unacknowledged hurts and latent misconceptions — it will all be there, waiting to be unpacked.

The choices we've made in our dating life can either bless our marriage—or rise up to haunt us.

If an understanding of what marriage is meant to be is clear in your mind, you stand a much better chance of making choices now that are consistent with that mental picture.

TIMELESS TRUTHS FROM A GARDEN WEDDING

If you want to view the state of the art of any item on the market today—whether computers, cameras, or microwave ovens—you search for the latest model. In the realm of human technology, the most recent design is the best. It's not that way with God. His original designs, whether they be a daisy, a baby, or a snowflake, are faultlessly perfect. Before there were parliaments and congresses, commerce and conglomerates, books, music, art, or systematic theology, God fashioned a woman from Adam's side, brought her to him, and declared openly His enormous pleasure as Matchmaker. Genesis 2:18-23 looks at the beginning of the most special of all human relationships—man and woman.

> The LORD God said, "It is not good for the man to be alone. I will make a helper suitable for him. . . .
>
> So the LORD God caused the man to fall into a deep sleep; and while he was sleeping, he took one of the man's ribs and closed up the place with flesh. Then the LORD God made a woman from the rib he had taken out of the man, and he brought her to the man.
>
> The man said, "This is now bone of my bones and flesh of my flesh; she shall be called 'woman,' for she was taken out of man."

FIRST THINGS FIRST

There is a sequence to these primal events that provides us something of a relational paradigm worthy of note. Adam first met his Master; his first and most important connection was a vertical one. That provided a kind of grounding from which anything else needful became possible. Then God gave him a mission in life, that of tending the garden. After that, God brought to Adam his *mate*. There is obvious wisdom to the way this story unfolds. It helps immensely to be centered in your relationship with Christ first, and to have some idea of the direction you are heading in life. Bringing a flesh-and-blood man or woman into that picture deepens and enriches each part.

GOD'S PROVISION FOR ADAM'S NEEDS

In this, the first of many marriages, God took the responsibility for providing the suitable bride. Adam's main job was to cooperate with God's plan; it's comforting to realize that God was the One who saw Adam's need. "It is not good for the man to be alone" (Genesis 2:18). While Adam was asleep and unaware, in what had to be the perfect timing, God provided the answer to Adam's need in the form of Eve.

In this case, God's response to man's lonely existence was to provide a woman, or as the text says, "a helper." (Marriage is not always God's answer to loneliness.) Since the word *helper* is often used in Scripture to refer to God Himself, the meaning is not degrading. "It conveys the idea of someone who 'assists another to reach complete fulfillment,'" says author Chuck Swindoll. "It is a beautiful picture of a dignified, necessary role filled by one whom God would make and bring alongside the man."[1]

Adam traded a rib for a wife. That was a profitable

trade, wouldn't you say? Certainly we see no evidence of regret as Adam exclaimed, "This is it!" (TLB). Adam recognized this woman to be exactly what he needed. Such a perfect creation as Eve revealed not only God's goodness but His intimate knowledge of Adam.

FOUR PRINCIPLES

Genesis 2:24-25 is not only God's commentary on the union of Adam and Eve, but also provides truths basic to any marriage. In a book that looks back to the first marriage, that of Adam and Eve, author Chuck Swindoll suggests that from these verses come four inviolable marriage principles.[2]

. . . a man shall leave his father and mother	SEVERANCE
. . . and shall cleave to his wife	PERMANENCE
. . . and they shall become one flesh	UNITY
. . . and the man and his wife were both naked and were not ashamed	INTIMACY

God doesn't offer an array of alternative lifestyles. Marriage is not a menu where you have a list of twenty-five possibilities from which to pick and choose. A man and woman come together, leaving their original families, to establish a union that brings forth children—and so the story continues yet another generation. But a man and woman united before Christ forms the heart of it all. Their lives are intertwined together spiritually, psychologically, emotionally, and physically as long as they live.

Perhaps you could parallel these principles to the process of coming to Christ. When we become His children through faith in the finished work of the cross, we in effect sever our ties with the world and cleave to Him. We grow in that unity and spiritual intimacy all the rest of our lives, until at long last, we dine with Him at the marriage feast of the Lamb (see Revelation 19:7-9).

GOD'S SEAL OF APPROVAL

"Marriage should be honored by all" (Hebrews 13:4). It's not that marriage is preferable necessarily to the single life, nor is it any higher calling. But marriage is special, as the Bible makes clear. The first institution was marriage; Christ's first miracle occurred at a wedding; the New Testament includes many instructions concerning the marriage relationship; and in eternity we will celebrate the marriage feast of the Lamb.

Marriage is the first holy relationship God ordained. Our human concept of holiness is that which is enshrined, or set apart as untouchable. God, however, takes eternal truths, for which we use the word *holy*, and places them in the living relationships of His people. The lifelong union of a man and a woman is holy because it symbolizes in human form the unseverable love of Christ for His bride, the church. Husbands are even encouraged to love their wives, *"as Christ loved the church and gave himself up for her"* (Ephesians 5:2,5; emphasis added).

Marriage in Christ is a privilege denied to angels and given only to men and women. Peter uses a beautiful phrase to describe it: fellow heirs of the grace of life (see 1 Peter 3:7). God takes the relationship so seriously that He warns husbands (in the same verse) that insensitive treatment of their wives may render their prayers ineffective. Likewise, wives are reminded that living in conflict with their husbands and rejecting their leadership brings dishonor to God's Word (Titus 2:5). Marriage in Christ is meant to be an undeniable example of a faith that works.

GIVING FLESH TO THE IDEAL

Does all this talk of marriage as something sacred, marriage as God intended it to be, sound like an unattainable ideal? After all, Christians sometimes have unhappy marriages. You probably know Christians who have divorced, Christians who have participated in adultery. The union of two individuals who know Christ is no guarantee of marital bliss—but it does provide the basis for something very special. What are some of the possible distinctives of a marriage that is grounded in Christ?

THE BASIS FOR FORGIVENESS

It is said that a good marriage is the union of two very good forgivers. Living closely with another person for a month, or a year . . . or for a lifetime means there are hundreds of opportunities to hurt each other. Some of those are minor irritations, everyday frustrations. And some of those are so deep, or so prolonged, that without the basis for forgiveness and starting over, two porcupines would have a better chance of keeping each other warm and cared for.

When we were first married, we found ourselves apologizing incredibly often, trying hard to keep short accounts between us. I remember looking at Stacy one day and admitting, "I had no idea, until I got married, that I was really a selfish person in so many ways." Stacy felt the same. We began to refer to each other, somewhat humorously, as "the big sinner" and "the little sinner." It was our way of acknowledging that we were two sinners who had married and would spend a lifetime learning to forgive well.

The gospel keeps us from being surprised by our own sin—or the sin of another. And the gospel gives us the basis on which to forgive, with grace enough for a lifetime.

A SET OF COMMON IDEALS

To make it for a lifetime, two individuals need a similar picture in their minds of what characterizes a good relationship. They have to know what they are aiming toward. Christianity provides the model for relationships, like a curtain you are invited to peek behind and see what's really there. In the model of the Trinity, the Father, the Son, and the Holy Spirit relate to each other in the closest of all contexts. What marks their relationship? Perhaps the best three words would be *respect, honor,* and *deference.* While the Bible speaks in specific terms to husbands and wives, still the essence of what makes a good marriage work can be summarized by those same three attributes: respect, honor, and deference. Christianity provides a couple with a common set of ideals.

STRENGTH GREATER THAN YOUR OWN

There are so many times, in the course of one lifetime, when only the supernatural will do. We have close friends who went to Colorado for a vacation recently, for instance. They could never have anticipated that, in a few moments' time, a simple bike ride would turn into the crisis of their lives. A reckless driver drove his car off the road and struck the husband while he was riding his bike. He lived, thanks to a ready air flight to a close trauma center, but he sustained significant head injuries.

The husband who greets his wife in the morning now looks very much the same—but there are differences only a wife would notice. Some of the traits in him she prized the most are no longer there. Perhaps they will return, but she has no guarantees. She is learning to love a man who is different from the one she remembers. In a moment's time, their lives together were altered—maybe irrevocably. How can any couple weather such an abrupt change in their own strength?

There is an old African proverb that states, "The earth was made round so that we would not see too far down the road." Life holds a collection of crises and tragedy, struggle and challenge that requires more than two people can give it. It requires strength greater than their own. The marriage of two Christians means that they have real and ready access to the power of God. Knowing this is the deepest form of security you can have in this life.

A CRUCIBLE OF GRACE
Marriage does provide, in its best moments, something of a sanctuary, refuge of safety and protection. But Christians know that marriage is also a crucible. It is a unique incubator of change and growth in which the One who made us shapes our character through the love—and the failure to love—of our mate. Martin Luther said that marriage was God's chosen school for building character into our lives.

Christianity is about this thing called transformation. God has promised that His love will mold the image of Christ in us. Christians have the advantage of knowing that marriage—as good as it can be, as painful as it can be—is a deep part of the process. We have less cause for surprise when things get rough. And we have more reason to hope.

WORTH THE PRICE
Do Christians who get married have an easier go of it? Not necessarily, we think. What we have is more opportunities to have a better go of it. The potential to experience something closer to what God had in mind is ours in fuller measure.

Usually, before Stacy and I drift off to sleep at night, we try to pray together. It's not a terribly spiritual exercise. We're tired, it's been a long day, there are all sorts of pressures in our lives. But often those moments crystallize for me the privilege of being two Christians called together in the journey of life in this thing called marriage. We are not alone. As rough as it can get—and as wonderful as it can be—we have the Lord, we have each other. *What a difference Christ has made in our lives.*

There is incredible potential in the union of two individuals who want to follow Christ. That's why the enemy of our souls works so hard on us, as single people, to steer us on another course. It's why Christian marriages sometimes experience what feels like shell and mortar attacks. A marriage grounded in Christ is a miniature drama of the love and grace of God. A marriage of two Christians influences generations of people to come.

For you personally, a clear understanding of marriage and how distinctive it can be between Christians, may well be the biggest motivation you have to make careful, prayerful choices in your relationships now. The goal must be clear in your mind. And it must be a worthy goal . . . one that is worth the pain, worth the price.

Notes
1. Charles R. Swindoll, *Strike the Original Match* (Portland, Oreg.: Multnomah, 1980), p. 19.
2. Swindoll, p. 21.

Questions for Personal Study and Application

1. How would you define marriage?
2. Read Genesis 2:18-25.
   a. What do you learn about men and women from this passage?
   b. Based on this passage, what is the marriage relationship to be like?
3. Read Ephesians 5:22-25.
   a. What instructions are given to the husband . . . to the wife?
   b. From this passage, what does a man's greatest need appear to be? A woman's?
   c. How does a woman show respect?
   d. What does it mean for a man to love his wife as Christ loved the Church?
4. Based on this passage, what are some things you would want to be true of your marriage?
5. What are some things you would want to be true of your future mate? Commit these to God in prayer.
6. What needs do you have that a spouse could minister to? What needs could you meet for a spouse?
7. What new commitments affecting dating and marriage will you make as a result of this study?
8. Write down any unanswered questions you may have on the marriage relationship.

Suggested Scripture Memory

Ephesians 5:33

Questions for Discussion

1. What major influences have had an effect on your concept of marriage?

2. Why is our culture so opposed to the biblical design for marriage? How would you paraphrase Ephesians 5:24-25?
3. How would you describe an ideal (biblical) relationship of a couple to their parents? Read Ephesians 5:18-21. What context is established there for verses 22-33? What are the characteristics of a spirit-filled life?
7. What new thoughts about marriage came to you from the Genesis 2 and Ephesians 5 passages?

CHAPTER THREE

Healthy Dating Relationships

૭ ૭ ૭

G oing out with someone — dating — in this day and time has become an amazingly complicated affair. It's best to state right up front that the Bible offers no set prescription for this thing we call dating. Marriages in those times were arranged by the family. How would you like to *begin* to get to know someone on the day you got married? That would give whole new meaning to the phrase, "nervous bride and groom." So we look to Scripture in this area, in terms of general principles.

The "rules" regarding dating change in every generation. Before the automobile became so common, couples got to know each other in the family parlor or during carefully supervised events. Through the years, a girl who asked a guy out would have been considered, in most situations, extremely brash. Until relatively recently, it was common to date a different person every night of the weekend; there was, in fact, a carefully orchestrated progression in moving from a casual relationship to one with serious potential. Casual dating now, in this era of AIDS and accelerated sexual involvement, is practically an oxymoron. It seems about as "casual" as a background check by the FBI. We are quickly losing the ease with which men and women, in generations past, got to know a fairly large selection of individuals in a fairly casual context, from which a few serious relationships occurred, and one of those ended in marriage.

Going out seems to be in a state of tremendous flux. Most Christians admit that there is still the expectation that men ask women out. They don't care how it's done on television—it's done differently in Christian circles. Still many of the standard signals—the way men and women communicate interest—have changed, or at least become confused. If it's not terribly clear who's supposed to ask who out—it's even less clear who should pick up the tab. And when the evening is over, who makes the first move to suggest getting together again? Women insist that if they're expected to pick up the phone and ask a guy out, they run a double risk. Not only may they encounter the guy's usual dilemma (they may be turned down), but they also run the risk of seeming pushy. As one woman said, "I feel like I may be putting an 'x' by my name if I take initiative toward a guy. I don't know what's appropriate." In some circles, the simple act of a guy and a girl going out together becomes a giant list of social transactions, each laden with heavy meaning. "Is it any wonder," one man said recently, "that a lot of us just don't go out with anyone?"

To which we say, "That's so sad." There shouldn't be so much riding on the whole experience of getting to know someone well—which is really what any form of dating is all about. Whether it's a group—or two individuals going out for an evening—the goal is to enjoy being with each other. And the goal is worth the effort.

Attitudes toward dating, now, come in every shape and size and variety. That's why it's even more important these days that you chart your own course in the direction you feel God is leading you. There are still updated versions of the old term "neverdaters"—those who hope that the love of their life will somehow just magically drop from the sky one day. On the opposite end of the spectrum there are singles who have been single far longer than they needed to be single. Their dating history holds a string of promising relationships—but with every year their standards rise. Yet another requirement is added to the list titled "suitable partner."

Recently, we heard the most novel approach yet to this whole conundrum of dating and marriage. In a recent book called *Marrying Smart*, the author advocates applying business principles to your personal life. She suggests that you go about this task in a direct way: make a list of the attributes desired in a partner, expose yourself to situations in which your gender is far outnumbered by the other gender, and set a date by which you want to be married. Our response was something akin to, "Whoa, doggies. Hold the fort!" If only relationships could be managed like a company's production line.

Our encouragement is that you give yourself some time to stand back and evaluate the whole question of how you relate to the opposite sex. What would "healthy dating relationships" look like in your life? How can dating be something that enriches your life—and the life of the person you go out with?

IMPORTANT REASONS TO DATE

Think, for a moment, about the purpose that something like dating is supposed to serve in your life. There are a number of ways that going out can represent a significant "growth opportunity."

TO DEVELOP SOCIALLY

Dating offers, potentially at least, some of life's choicest moments to grow in social skills. On the face of things, that's rather obvious. Going out with someone is about relating—no matter how sophisticated or mundane the activity. Yet we find that the significance of this kind of personal growth is easily overlooked. In fact, most of us come into the relational world expecting to be experts—suave, confident, knowledgeable from the start. One professor of psychiatry at Brown University admitted that most of the students he counseled sought help with anxiety around their relationships with the opposite sex. He claimed they had an "unrealistic perception of what occurs on dates so they can never live up to their expectations."[1] It seems that knowing how to plan for a date, what to say and do, and how to initiate and maintain conversation can be overwhelming obstacles for many people.

Some people never confront their anxiety, and simply shy away from the prospect of going out much. Others rely on a crutch to make them feel comfortable socially. Alcohol has long been the most common pacifier of social anxiety, since it appears to embolden even the shyest with a measure of confidence. And have you ever considered how much sexual involvement is an escape from the harder task of *really* getting to know someone? It's possible to rely on those two crutches and never make much progress in learning the fine art of relating to a man or woman well. The truth is that feeling comfortable with the opposite sex is a process, something that takes time and courage to learn.

Even Christ developed socially over a period of time, the Bible tells us. He "grew in wisdom and stature, and in favor with God and men" (Luke 2:52). That takes some of the pressure off all of us to have to be experts in areas of life where there's no substitute for time and attentiveness.

Really feeling comfortable with the opposite sex means being able to make someone else feel at ease. It's about being able to put your own anxiety aside, at least for a while.

To Grow in Character

The most common approach to going out with someone is to place the emphasis on externals. For instance, when we were giving seminars on this topic regularly, we usually asked the group to describe what they considered to be the ideal date. We were amazed at the consistency of the response. No matter what part of the country or what the group was like, the answers were fairly much the same. The group would come forth with an image of an attractive man or woman in a sharp-looking car taking off for some place everyone would want to go. It was evident that the same set of magazine advertisements and television commercials are imprinted on all our brains.

If we can just get past the images, though, we know intuitively that relationships—the real ones, at least—are about something else. Something entirely different. We would like to suggest to you that much of that difference is contained in the word *character.* Character is the inner substance you reveal when you respond selflessly to another person. Let us take a moment to explain.

In every potentially close relationship, especially those between men and women, there is a wild card present. It's part of the chemistry of attraction between two people. And it's also what makes things a bit scary. The wild card is one of risk: *Can I take the risk to let myself be known by another person? I could experience something really good in this relationship. Or I could get hurt. I could end up putting my heart on the line and getting it trounced.* There are no guarantees in relationships, not in the real ones anyway.

A young engineer in his twenties shared with me the story of what he'd learned about taking risks in a relationship. He had finally found a girl he enjoyed so much that he began to think, *I could see myself spending a lifetime with this person.* It was like they were reading off the same page—she could complete his sentences, so similar was their thinking. In popular jargon, they really connected. One day she came to him and said what he had never anticipated hearing. "I'm sorry, Doug," she said. "There are some issues in my past that keep getting in the way. I can't go any further in this relationship. I can't see you any more." And that was it. Doug was left, not only with the pain and loss, but wondering what had happened.

He chose to write her a letter in which he told her how much the relationship meant to him and what it was in her he so enjoyed, and leave it at that. I wish I could say that she at least answered his letter, but she didn't. Months later I asked Doug if he was glad he'd written her, even though he received no response. He said it was good to get on paper the way he felt, to at least take the opportunity to share his heart. I could only admire his courage. Taking those kinds of vulnerable risks in a relationship requires tremendous character.

Going out with someone, whether it's a serious relationship or not, is a ripe opportunity to grow in character. Dating provides the chance to develop sensitivity to someone else's frame of reference. "Do nothing from selfishness or empty conceit, but with humility of mind let each of you regard one another as more important than himself," Paul said (Philippians 2:3, NASB). Being willing to take risks, putting the other person first—these are some of the ways in which dating relationships stretch and develop our character.

Character, which is really about the capacity to give and receive love, is invaluable. It's priceless. "How much better it is to get wisdom than gold! And to get understanding is to be chosen above silver" (Proverbs 16:16, NASB). Character is the real capital we carry into a long-term relationship like marriage.

MARKS OF A HEALTHY RELATIONSHIP

We would not want to leave the impression that going out with someone—the simple act of dating—is a particularly weighty affair. In fact, a common refrain we often hear is the complaint that no one just goes out to have a good time anymore. "I can't just call up a girl and say, 'Let's go rollerblading and get some ice cream,'" one friend complained. "I don't know what she'll read into that invitation." It's as though there is too much riding on the event.

Dating is really founded on friendships. The best long-term relationships actually grow out of having been good friends first. If you are new into this thing of being a Christian, you may want to take a period of time in which you pull back from going out and reevaluate your relationships with the opposite sex altogether. But after that, you want to enjoy getting to know as many people as God realistically makes possible. There shouldn't be so much at stake in the simple act of dating.

Having said that, it's important to know what distinguishes a good relationship—the healthy kind—from those that are not what the doctor ordered, so to speak. Here are some of the marks of what you might call "healthy dating relationships."

A SHARED SENSE OF STEWARDSHIP

What if we told you that there is one spiritual truth which once embraced, in and of itself, would revolutionize the way you saw relationships with the opposite sex? Brace yourself, this one is deceptively simple. *You and every person you date are made in the image of God, valued beyond belief, purchased with the blood of Christ. You are, in fact, brothers and sisters in His family.*

Do you see what we mean? If that's really true, then how could we be dishonest or seductive or inconsiderate in a relationship, and not feel the cleansing stab of real guilt? It changes everything, suddenly, if you are brothers and sisters in Christ first—even before you are friends and long before you are lovers (married ones, of course). A healthy relationship—the good, life-giving kind—grows out of a sense of stewardship, each for the other. We are our brother's keeper, the Bible says.

Now this is just plain different from the way the world does relationships, and it was meant to be as radical as it sounds. Two individuals normally circle each other in a relationship asking, in unspoken words, "What can I *get* from you that I need?" Men tend to seek sexual conquest. Woman are often in search of security, especially the emotional kind. Consciously or unconsciously, they try to tilt the scales in their direction to meet their own needs. Both parties seem to ask, "How can I get you to mirror back to me what a desirable person I am?" Hence, the pull and tug of many relationships between the sexes.

In a healthy relationship, the two individuals going out have shifted the focus more toward giving—and away from just getting their own needs met. There is an acceptance of responsibility for the other person's welfare as well. One new Christian in his thirties said to us, "The biggest change in my relationships with women is that I am able to come to the relationship without my own needs dictating the picture. I'm able to *give* out of the substance of my life in Christ." You can often measure the quality of a relationship in terms of the degree to which this sense of stewardship is present.

GENTLE HONESTY

Relationships that are redemptive—rather than exploitative or manipulative—are always marked by this attribute of honesty. How could you ever learn to trust someone you weren't sure could shoot straight with you? And trust is the fundamental currency of good relationships.

Sometimes when I hear dating couples discuss their relationships, I am reminded of that backyard mole we used to see in cartoons as children. Here, there, and everywhere—you never knew which hole the mole would stick his head up from. Relationships that are better lost than kept often have this deceptive quality to them. Words are said—then taken back. Or what someone does is nearly contrary to what they claimed. The dance between the two individuals is crazy because too often, "yes" doesn't mean "yes" and "no" doesn't mean "no," as Christ instructed us. One or both individuals just get jerked around.

Keeping a relationship honest requires a commitment to checking in with each other whenever one person or the other feels in the dark.

One couple we knew, Bill and Amanda, had been going out for a while and just by the nature of things, Bill picked up the tab. They had a great time together. But then the relationship began to cool: their spiritual backgrounds were just too different, their personalities didn't quite gel. He wanted to take a job in another state. And so . . . without talking much about the obvious, Bill signaled his own change of heart by the simple act of letting Amanda pay her way. It took Amanda's commitment to being up front and aboveboard to eventually say, "Uh, Bill, something is different here. I'm fine about paying my way, but it seems like you are trying to tell me something. What is it?" That's the kind of honesty that keeps things real.

A COMMITMENT TO MUTUAL GROWTH

In a wonderful passage about relationships in the book of Ephesians, Paul encourages his audience to watch carefully the words they say. Only say those things that build another person up, "according to the need of the moment, that it may give grace to those who hear" (Ephesians 4:29). The emphasis is on doing whatever is necessary in a relationship to build up the other person, spiritually and emotionally.

In college, I spent a number of months going out with a Lebanese Christian. He eventually became a good friend. I lost track of the hours we talked over coffee, in which he tried to open up my small-town frame of reference so that I could actually see the challenges and possibilities in the Middle East. His heart for the world was absolutely contagious. I am blessed, years later even, from his influence. I was "built up" just by knowing him.

Relationships among Christians are often pictured as a triangle. The man and the woman stand at the bottom corners of the triangle. At the top is God. The idea depicted is that as each person moves closer to God, they will move closer to each other as well. The focus for each individual is the Lord.

Because you are a Christian, God really is in the picture in your relationships with the opposite sex. It's not just wishful thinking. Since He is present, the relevant question is whether the relationship is drawing you closer to Him. Are you a help or a hindrance to the person you are going out with—and he with you? Do you find yourself, at the end of an evening, feeling challenged and encouraged? Could you look back after six months of going out with someone and say, "I really grew spiritually in my walk with God and as a man or woman during the time I knew. . . ." Healthy relationships have this quality of encouraging mutual growth.

USING DISCERNMENT

No book on relationships with the opposite sex, written for a Christian audience, would be complete without posing the question: how much difference does it make if you date—or even marry—a nonChristian?

More than you might think, actually. This is one issue on which the Bible is clear. In fact, the classic passage on this subject, 2 Corinthians 6:14-18, is like a wake-up call. Marrying a person who is not really and truly a Christian is one of the few things in the world of relationships in which Scripture plainly says, DON'T DO THAT! Let's take a look at the passage in 2 Corinthians.

> Do not be yoked together with unbelievers. For what do righteousness and wickedness have in common? Or what fellowship can light have with darkness? What harmony is there between Christ and Belial? What does a believer have in common with an unbeliever? What agreement is there between the temple of God and idols? For we are the temple of the living God. As God has said: "I will live with them and walk among them, and I will be their God, and they will be my people.
>
> "Therefore come out from them and be separate, says the Lord. Touch no unclean thing, and I will receive you.
>
> "I will be a Father to you, and you will be my sons and daughters, says the Lord Almighty."
> (2 Corinthians 6:14-18)

For starters, marriage is designed for oneness. So the marriage of a believer and an unbeliever can never get quite where it's supposed to go. It's self-defeating from the start.

It's like mixing oil and water—or as the passage indicates, light and darkness, Christ and Belial, the temple of God and idols. Those are strong words. The picture of a Christian yoked together with a nonChristian gives new meaning to the phrase "coming from different places."

The Scriptural metaphor used here is that of two oxen, unequally yoked. Old Testament law forbade such a practice. It wasn't fair to the oxen. And you simply couldn't plow a straight row with two animals not designed to fit the same yoke, each drawn to go off in his own direction. "Being unequally yoked" is a way of describing the chafing frustration of being with someone—day in and day out—whose values and outlook on life are, by the nature of things, very different from yours.

Similarly, the Bible says when we come to Christ, the actual love of God is poured out in our heart (Romans 5:5). A mate who is an unbeliever cannot return that in kind. Consequently, what most couples report in marriages in which one of them is not yet a believer is a kind of heart-rending loneliness—loneliness at a soul level.

It's one thing for a couple to marry as nonChristians and then one, but not both, come to Christ. It's quite another, as a single person, to just turn a blind eye to the real question of your partner's spirituality, hoping that after marriage it will magically work out. "Love is blind but marriage is a great eye-opener," Abraham Lincoln once said. And a lack of genuine commitment to Christ before marriage is not likely to reverse itself after the honeymoon. As most counselors and pastors will tell you, a spiritually-mixed marriage is usually a prescription for loneliness and frustration.

Dating nonChristians, for all the reasons above, is skating on thin relational ice. The biggest problem with it is that it's just too easy to fall in love! And then what do you do? I am always reminded of the morning I opened my front door to a friend I hadn't seen in a year. Pain creased the lines in her face. She wanted to talk. It was about a man she rode to work with, someone she'd gotten to know. At first, he was just a friend, a rather interesting man, with interesting ideas, none of which leaned toward Christianity. Then they had begun to go out—more and more often. Now she was in a terrible place because her heart was torn—she loved this man and she wanted to follow Christ. She felt split in half.

I wish this kind of story were more uncommon. It's because of this kind of heartache that most people will say to you: if you want to avoid some pain, if you want to marry a Christian, date within the Christian community. Put a potential mate's spiritual commitment at the top of your list of "must have" attributes.

Most single individuals who end up "unequally yoked" to someone have fallen prey to a similar process. They go out with someone and rationalize away the lack of spiritual commitment that's evidenced. They engage in a lot of wishful thinking. "Sally is such a thoughtful woman. She's nicer than many Christians I know! It will all come together for her spiritually in time, I'm sure." As they get more emotionally involved, they become even less discerning. Too often, the relationship eventually sinks to the level of the lowest spiritual common denominator. The person with the least commitment and spiritual interest ends up exerting the greater influence. And a marriage that is less than it was meant to be takes place.

As you look at God's instructions in 2 Corinthians on the subject of marrying a nonChristian, you will notice a remarkable promise at the end of that passage. God calls us, as believers, to a way of life that will make us different from those around us. At times we will feel the pang of that difference—perhaps especially in the area of intimate relationships. But God promises that in this place of choosing to go a different path—one that seems initially harder—He will meet you Himself. "I will be a Father to you, and you will be my sons and daughters" (verse 18). He provides His own special intimacy in those painful places.

WITH ONE EYE TO THE FUTURE

Dating as a single person is much like driving with one eye on the road ahead, and one eye on the person in the front seat beside you. Both the present and the future clamor for your attention. You must develop the discernment to see how your choices now can and will affect your life down the road. And all the while, there is the reality of asking the Lord, "How are You leading me?"

Our encouragement to you is to make the connection between your life now, as a single person, and your probable marriage in the future. You won't wake up on your honeymoon and be a different person—more considerate, less selfish, more skilled at relating well. Your fears and insecurities will follow you, for the most part, down the aisle. The way you've learned to relate to men or women, in all those years of dating, will influence your capacity to give and receive love later. Your character, formed by your heart for God and your sensitivity to others, will be the most valuable asset you have to offer anyone.

Let's continue to look at relationships among Christians by looking at the way our gender—maleness and femaleness—affects the way we relate.

Note
1. As reported by Marilyn Machlowitz in "Anxiety Still Surrounds U.S. Dating Practices," *Stillwater News Press*, 19 May 1981, p. 8.

Questions for Personal Study and Application

1. What attitudes and behaviors characterize dating in our culture now?
2. According to the following passages, how are two believers to relate to each other?
   a. Our attitudes: Romans 12:10, 14:13; Ephesians 4:2.
   b. Our actions: Romans 14:19; Galatians 5:13, 6:2.
   c. Our speech: Colossians 3:9,16; 1 Thessalonians 5:11.
3. What good purposes has dating served in your life?
4. Look at Paul's words directed to relationships in general within the Body of Christ, as written in Ephesians 4:25-32. What principles do you see and how do they apply to your relationships with the opposite sex?
5. Study 2 Corinthians 6:14-18. What are the differences between Christians and nonChristians? How would these differences affect a marriage relationship or a business partnership, for example?
6. As you reflect on this chapter, what do you most feel needs to change about your relationships with the opposite sex? What are you encouraged by?

Suggested Scripture Memory

Pick your favorite selection from the verses in question 2 and commit it to memory.

Questions for Discussion

1. What good purposes should dating fill in a believer's life?
2. How should a dating relationship between two believers be different?
3. Some additional verses to read are Romans 12:16 and

15:7, Ephesians 4:31, and Hebrews 3:13. What are practical examples of ways to apply these verses in dating situations?

4. How might these specific differences affect a date, and how should you respond to them?

5. Summarize what you think are the marks of a healthy dating relationship.

CHAPTER FOUR

Natural Symmetry

⊃ ⊃ ⊂

> There are three things that are too amazing for me,
> four that I do not understand: the way of an eagle in
> the sky, the way of a snake on a rock, the way of a
> ship on the high seas, and the way of a man with a
> maiden. (Proverbs 30:18-19)

Like an eagle or a snake or a ship, a relationship between a man and woman is at once a mysterious and a beautiful thing. It's like watching the characters in a drama—except that it's real life! Each one has his or her own lines to say and a complementary part to play in the life of the other. The unfolding of each character determines whether you view a masterpiece production or a disaster-in-the-making.

Yet we live in a culture where people get nervous anytime someone hints at the obvious: men and women are different. The fear is that acknowledging those differences will be used as a way to justify unfair and unequal treatment, especially for women. Equality will get lost in the shuffle.

Once again, the Scriptures move beyond this narrow debate. In the New Testament, the basis for equality was never dependent on being the same. There's no need to nullify differences between the sexes because our equality—a sense of equal worth—resides in our shared spiritual standing before God. Peter says that men and women are heirs together of "the grace of life" (1 Peter 3:7, NASB). In the very beginning God created man in His image—His image bearing all the aspects of being male and female (Genesis 1:27). How can one gender be "more valuable" than the other if all the attributes of both are part of God Himself?

It's precisely Scripture's insistence in the worth and equal value of both sexes that lets us look freely at our differences. When we fail to appreciate those differences—when we try to pretend men and women are the same—we deprive each other of some part of the "glory" God gave each sex in creation. Walter Trobisch, one of the first and best writers on men and women's relationships from a Christian perspective, once said, "The woman can only be a woman as long as a man is a man. And the man can only be a man as long as a woman is a woman. When you even out the differences, you deprive them both."[1]

We have to ask ourselves what sexuality is all about, at its essence. Are there differences in the software (the way we think and relate) or only differences in the hardware (physical attributes)?

We want to pose for you that being made, male and female, in the image of God profoundly influences the way we think and act and move about in the world. Those differences may be hard to put into words sometimes and over-generalizing is always a danger. But differences nonetheless there are—moreover, they are a cause worth celebrating!

That men and women come from such different places

is what makes relationships frustrating at times—but it adds spice and intrigue too. It's why we form an unbeatable combination when we are able to capitalize on each other's unique orientation to life.

NATURAL SYMMETRY

Numerous studies point to evidence that differences between men and women can be observed early on—as early as the hospital nursery, even. At that tender age, baby girls track pictures of people's faces longer and more intently than do baby boys, while boys are more active physically. By the time we reach elementary school, the difference in the way boys and girls relate to life shows up in other ways. One fascinating study was first reported by Carol Gilligan, in her landmark book *In a Different Voice*.[2] When arguments arose during the course of play on an elementary playground, observers noticed that the boys' groups had a different way of dealing with the impasse: they quickly resolved the dispute and got back to the game. Finishing the game was the big deal. Girls' groups were more willing to disband the activity entirely so they could devote their attention to restoring harmony to the relationships. The subject of attention and motivation seems to vary between boys and girls with notable consistency.

As adults, these same differences are observable in different ways. Women's style of relating focuses more on intimacy and connectedness.[3] Deborah Tannen, a social linguist, wrote that women often see themselves as individuals in a "network of connections . . . [where life] is a community, a struggle to preserve intimacy and avoid isolation."[4] A man, however, engages the world as an individual in a social order that is hierarchical, where he is either one-up or one-down. "Conversations are negotiations in which people try to achieve and maintain the upper hand if they can. . . . Life, then, is a contest, a struggle to preserve independence and avoid failure."[5] Tannen's assessment is that "though all humans need both intimacy and independence, women tend to focus on the first and men on the second. *It is as if their lifeblood ran in different directions*"[6] (emphasis added).

While some people see gender as a cage, a trap that needs to be sprung, gender differences contain the kernel of what makes relationships between men and women special. In those differences we find the basis for our own unique *potential* and our *responsibility* to each other, as men and women created in His image.

WHAT WOMEN BRING TO THE PICTURE

At the risk of over-generalizing, it seems that women are more attuned to people, as though indeed they have been watching their faces for a very, very long time. Women often pick up the gestures, subtle connotations, and nuances of words that tell you what's *really* happening. Their outlook on life tends to be more subjective and emotional—they readily assess a situation or a decision in terms of its impact on people. Men, as Tannen notes, are more attuned to achievement and task.

That's all just interesting information—until you try to combine those different styles in a relationship. Then it can get pretty wild! Picture George and Sarah, for a moment, who have gone out with another couple for dinner. They've only been out a few times, and they have a movie to make by 7:30. Sarah is eating slowly because she's busy—she's engaged in noticing that the couple they're with isn't getting along tonight. Could they be on the verge of breaking up, she wonders? Things don't look good. But George is not registering much of the tension in the air, really. His concern is whether he's going to get this group finished in time to catch the movie.

Scenes like this are just a part of life—George is really missing what's happening between this couple and Sarah will miss the movie unless she hurries a bit. *These natural differences are what makes each sex the natural complement for the other*. Both sides of the coin are terribly needed. The most significant thing that men and women, guys and girls bring to each other in a relationship is a measure of comfortableness with who they are as individuals—men and women—secure in Christ. From that vantage point, they are free to enjoy the difference in the other person.

Every guy can benefit from a girl's perspective on life— that seems obvious. But many women don't realize that they offer men something else, not readily seen, but very important. Women offer men an opportunity to shoulder responsibility. Let us explain.

As we close the century, the tables have turned between the sexes. Women pay their own way on dates. Women often make the plans and the arrangements for going out. In a large percentage of the couples who went to the prom in our daughter's high school last year, for instance—the girl asked the guy to be her escort for the evening. Mothers of adolescent guys complain regularly about the number of girls calling their sons. The term tossed about in secular media is "aggressive females." That guys, men, should actually be expected to exercise a muscle called *initiative* is supposedly a throwback to the horse-and-buggy era. Women can do that just as well as men. Some guys even like it that way—no need to worry over those awkward moments of being turned down.

Notice, though, the other cry rising from women these days. "Where are the men?" "Why are men so passive?" The sad part is that we often don't connect the first part of the equation with the second. Guys learn to be the men we need them to be by shouldering responsibility and assuming the risks entailed in exercising initiative from early on. Perhaps the best word would be a paraphrase of an old one: *Don't steal their thunder!* You serve a guy best if, as a woman, you hold on to your expectation that the role of initiative is one *he* needs to exercise.

It's no coincidence that God refers to Himself with a masculine pronoun—and the hallmark of His relationship with us is that He moved toward us first. He exercised the initiative. God is so masculine, C. S. Lewis once noted, that the whole of creation is feminine in comparison to Him. He pursues us as tenaciously as any lover ever could. In their relationship with men, women feel this same longing to be pursued. To keep that hope alive, though, they have to leave the uncomfortable space in place—and let a man get the picture that he needs to take the lead.

Having said that, though, a man needs some encouragement, some sign that his interest is reciprocal! One friend of ours, John, related how smitten he was with a girl his sophomore year in college. They went out a few times and he let it drop after that. He didn't think she was all that interested. Imagine his disappointment when she admitted two years later, once she was engaged to someone else, that "she'd really had a big crush on him when they were sophomores!" Either she didn't know how to convey her interest—or he wasn't able to read it.

Have you ever considered what an interesting example the Old Testament character of Ruth makes in this kind of discussion? Perhaps you remember her story. Ruth was a woman with some spine—she chose to go back to the place of her mother-in-law's birth when she could have stayed in the known and familiar. She faced famine, the loneliness of widowhood, and the depression of her mother-in-law. She eventually married Boaz and the circumstances surrounding that relationship are worth noting. The Bible says that she went in one night and lay down at the foot of where Boaz was sleeping. When he awakened, he recognized her and the love story goes on from there. If you look at the story as a metaphor, you see that Ruth made herself available. There was no hint of subservience or seductiveness in her act. She simply made herself available to Boaz, knowing that the real initiative in the relationship was his to take.

"A man needs a woman," writes Richard Robertiello, "who will affirm his masculine power, enjoy it, enhance it and get something from it, rather than envy it and try to destroy it."[7] Women bring to a relationship, not only their unique perspective on life—but the opportunity to let a man be a man, to let a guy be a guy—and both enjoy the benefits.

THE DARK SIDE OF FEMININE INFLUENCE

Out of his experience with 700 wives and 300 concubines, King Solomon penned his impressions about women. More than two thousand years later we still read what he wrote and recognize the words of a wise man. Certainly he was around enough women to make some careful observations! "I find more bitter than death," he wrote, "the woman who is a snare, whose heart is a trap and whose hands are chains" (Ecclesiastes 7:26).

All of those word pictures—a snare, a trap, chains— speak of the quality of manipulation and seductiveness that can creep into our relationships with men. We are talking about all the subtle and not-so-subtle means a woman has at her disposal to bind a guy's affections to her. Proverbs speaks of the adulterous woman, "the strange woman . . . who flatters with her words" (Proverbs 2:16, NASB). It says she uses her eyes in ways that lure men (Proverbs 6:25). The emphasis in these classic passages is on manipulation—doing whatever it takes to pull a guy in.

Sometimes women are conscious of being seductive—and the prize just seems to justify the chase. Especially if there's been a real lack of male attention and affection from a girl's father as she is growing up, the need to fill that absence can be enormous. And sometimes a woman is not aware of what motivates her—she hasn't connected the way she dresses or comes on to a guy with something that's harmful to them both. She just sees something she wants.

The tendency is for guys to give love—in order to get sex. And just the reverse is true for girls: women usually give sex to get love. Kelly was a woman in her twenties that we got to know while she was part of a singles fellowship. She also taught school. We went for months without seeing her until one day, she came by. Instantly, I thought, *She must have some physical problem. Or maybe her class is unusually difficult this year.* Her face looked so drawn and tired.

The story that came pouring out was that she had gone against all her values and let a guy move in with her because she was convinced they would get married the following summer. She had given sex to get love. She had been ensnared, really, by her own illusions, that a physical relationship would be enough to bind his heart to her for the long haul. Disappointment was written all over her.

The dark side of feminine influence—seductiveness and manipulativeness—are radically altered if we are free enough to see a man first *as a brother*. Romans 14:13 admonishes, "Make up your mind not to put any stumbling block or obstacle in your brother's way." If a guy is really a brother first, then your motivation will be to do whatever honestly serves him.

WHAT MEN BRING TO THE PICTURE

Each sex has its own particular risks to face. Guys fear having their advances rebuffed and rejected. Women struggle with the fear of not being chosen, of being perceived as undesirable. Each sex also carries its own benefits or privileges. Men are more aggressive, exploratory, dominant, and muscular.[8] Historically, they have enjoyed the cultural advantages associated with "male privilege." But being a woman has its own unique privilege as well. What achievement can begin to compare, for instance, with the potential every woman has to bring forth life itself?

In his book about men and women, George Gilder explains that in childbearing or the potential for childbearing, "Every woman is capable of a feat of creativity and durable accomplishment—permanently and uniquely changing the face of the earth—that only the most extraordinary man can even pretend to duplicate in external activity."[9]

As men begin to consider their role and responsibility in a woman's life, they come to something of an internal crossroads. That crossroads presents a choice. Will a man focus his energy on contributing to a woman's growth—that which is in her best interest—or will he use his influence to control and conquer? What can a guy contribute to the life of a girl he's going out with?

For one thing, it helps if a guy is willing to run counter to some of the classic stereotypes. Instead of letting her do the talking, for instance, learn what it is to carry the weight of a significant conversation. The tendency for men is to rely on touch to communicate, rather than words. But when a man talks, when he is free to share his thoughts, and when he's able to draw out a woman, she hears much more than words. She hears that she's valued.

Many girls grow up rating their physical appearance on an invisible scale from one to ten they're convinced exists in every man's head. I heard one woman laugh about the fraternity house she walked by on her daily stroll to class, where the guys lined the front porch and called out a number for every girl who came past. Imagine watching someone size you up and then hearing "She's a four" announced to everyone with ears! This woman claimed that after a while she would beat them to the punch line. She'd survey the bodies lining the porch and call out her own number first.

Real communication — talking about what's real in your life or hers — tells a woman that she's important because she's herself. Appearance, status, achievement, all these things are secondary.

In conversation, it's the little things that matter. Can you, for instance, ask open-ended questions? That sounds a bit too simple, but you wouldn't believe how often we hear people say something like, "Well, I enjoyed going out with . . . . But you know, they pretty much just talked about themselves all night. They never asked me the first question." And being able to reflect what you heard her say (reflective listening) sounds simple, but you wouldn't believe how seldom it's done. "Oh, you mean your job's in jeopardy and you're feeling really anxious." Most of us grossly underestimate how much it means to feel even the slightest measure of being understood by another human being. That's what taking the time to really listen and reflect does in a conversation.

When you're talking with a woman, it's important to cover both thoughts and feelings. Not one or the other, necessarily, but both whenever possible. That can cut down on volumes of misunderstanding. Especially in heavy duty conversations, talking about thoughts and feelings is crucial. I remember asking a friend, Eleanor, about the man she had been seeing for a number of months. She looked at the floor and said, "Well, I guess you could say that one's history." I asked her what had happened. Apparently, Jim just announced one day that he didn't think the relationship had a future. Things just weren't clicking.

"So did you talk it through?" I asked. "Did you at least share what you thought or how it all affected you?"

"He didn't ask and I didn't say," she replied. "We just left it at that." Relationships—and even good conversations—ought to have a reciprocal feel to them. There needs to be plenty of give and take.

Women also long to feel that, when it comes to a man she's getting to know, she can count on him. He's in her court, on her team; he assumes some responsibility for her best interest, even in the most casual of relationships. That must be a confusing message to men today who have grown up hearing the feminist slogan, "A woman needs a man like a fish needs a bicycle." Women don't like to admit that they need a man—that it feels good to have someone look out for them.

This dynamic is clearer in married couples but it applies more broadly. If you're talking with a married couple who's struggling, it is common to ask the wife if she feels protected by her husband—cared for and cherished. That question strikes so deep at a woman's longings that it almost always elicits tears. The summer that Stacy and I met, he was working at a construction site with rather rough guys who kept pornography in their trucks. When I offered to pick him up on-site to ride in the daily carpool, he responded that he'd rather walk down the hill. He didn't want me around that scene. "It's no place for a woman," he said. I knew instantly and I was right—here was a guy with some strength who was genuinely looking out for my best interests. I knew I could trust him.

It's a challenge to interpret the signals that men and women give each other these days. One almost-engaged couple related to us an amusing story that could have ended their relationship early on. When Harry began to date Celeste, she noticed that every door they came to, he let her open it for herself. "Once we went through a whole shopping center with me opening one door after another," she says. Because Harry was raised by a strong mother in a rather feminist atmosphere, he assumed that opening doors would seem insulting to a woman. He thought it was important not to act like a woman might actually need his help. And what was Celeste thinking, as she opened all her own doors? That Harry was insensitive, even disrespectful. That Harry didn't really care about her! If they hadn't talked about their perceptions, they would have missed each other by a mile.

Sigmund Freud once noted that after thirty years of study and exploration into the feminine psyche he was still trying to answer this most basic question, "What exactly does a woman want?" It must be even more confusing to men these days. They're told they need to be more sensitive . . . but not too much. Weakness, passivity has no big draw. They're told to take more initiative . . . but not be pushy and aggressive.

In the midst of such conflicting messages, though, two qualities emerge supreme. At the risk of preempting Freud's search, it seems that what a woman instinctively longs for is *a combination of warmth and strength*. And those are traits that can be seen, in stunning clarity, all through the life of Christ. As we follow Him, He molds us into men who can use our heads—and trust our hearts; men who know how to lead—and aren't afraid to follow when need be; men who can speak the truth—and say it with love.

THE DARK SIDE OF MASCULINITY

Many people grow up with a distorted view of masculinity that equates sexual appeal and conquest with being a man. Few of us are immune to that pressure. As one guy said to us, "By the time I was a freshman in college, I could always expect other guys to ask me if I was sleeping with the girl I was dating. The idea of purity was puritanical. Even worse, it meant being weak." The dark side of masculinity pressures a man to use a woman to prove something about himself.

In Proverbs 31, we find a passage often quoted to women, a line-by-line description of an excellent woman, a virtuous one. Did you know, though, that the first ten verses are addressed to men? They give the rest of the story. They reveal the pitfalls men can fall into—and the pathway out. Essentially, they tell *how to be a man who deserves a good woman*.

The first instruction is not too surprising. "Do not give your strength to women, or your ways to that which destroys kings" (Proverbs 31:3, NASB). In other words, don't be a skirt chaser. Don't give your strength as a man to sensuality. Lesser transgressions have ruined greater men than you. Somehow a man must first gain control of his own impulse and appetite before he can gain control of more complicated matters in his life. Paul phrases this idea rather poetically. Each person, he says, must know "how to possess his own vessel in sanctification and honor, not in lustful passion . . ." (1 Thessalonians 4:4-5, NASB).

The rest of the passage cautions against giving in to "strong drink" (verses 4-9) when there are so many needs of those less fortunate. The picture is that of not letting external influences overpower your senses so that your real responsibilities go begging. So much in this world depends on you. If you would find a pathway through the pitfalls of your nature, then find your mission in life. Give your strength to Kingdom purposes.

GREAT POTENTIAL, GREAT RESPONSIBILITY

Men and women, as they date and marry or just relate day to day, have so much influence in each other's lives—more influence than they realize. In every encounter we can leave each other a bit more blessed—or a bit more bruised.

God calls us to take the uniqueness of our sexuality— our maleness and femaleness—and use it for each other's good. Whether we are single or married, none of us lives or dies to himself. We belong to each other. We are not our own. For though we are many, we are all part of His body, "and individually members one of another" (Romans 12:5, NASB).

Notes
1. Walter Trobisch, "Lovestyle," *His*, February 1975, p. 25.
2. Carol Gilligan, *In a Different Voice* (Boston: Harvard University Press, 1982).
3. Deborah Tannen, *You Just Don't Understand* (New York: Ballantine Books, 1990).
4. Tannen, p. 26.
5. Tannen, p. 25.
6. Tannen, p. 26.
7. Richard Robertiello, source unknown.
8. George Gilder, *Men and Marriage* (Gretna, La.: Pelican Publishing, 1989), p. 20.
9. Gilder, p. 18.

Questions for Personal Study and Application

1. Describe in your own words how men and women are different and how that difference affects relationships.
2. In the classic passage given to wives and husbands, 1 Peter 3:1-10 (NASB), Peter uses that phrase, "fellow-heir of the grace of life." Are there principles and insights in this passage that have bearing on the way you treat each other, even as single men and women, and if so, what are they?
3. Look at the following verses, which give insight into the darker side of male-female relationships. What insights do you gather? Proverbs 2:16-19, 9:13-15, 27:15-16.
4. Look up the phrase "one another" in a concordance. Find as many responsibilities that each of us has to the other as you can. How would you apply these to a dating relationship?
5. Read the whole chapter of Proverbs 31. What traits, as a man or a woman, do you feel led to pray that God would develop in your life? What attributes would you hope/pray for in the life of the man or woman you marry?

Suggested Scripture Memory

Philippians 2:3-4

Questions for Discussion

1. Why does it usually feel like a "touchy subject" to talk about men and women as though they were actually different? How do you see those differences?
2. What role should physical attractiveness play in your attraction to a particular guy or girl?

3. How have you been blessed by a particular guy or girl . . . or bruised?
4. Are you aware of how you have hurt someone in a relationship? Are you aware of how you've helped or blessed them?
5. Read 1 Peter 3:8-12. How can you apply these verses to your relationships with the opposite sex?
6. Complete this sentence and discuss: "If I actually saw the guy or girl I went out with as a brother or sister in Christ first, before I considered them in a more romantic light, that would change the way I related to them in these ways. . . ."

CHAPTER FIVE

Why Not?

◯ ◯ ◯

A professor at Duke University, Hornell Hart, used to tell his classes that the survival of the human race depended on three things. "We have to (a) get our breakfast, (b) avoid being someone else's breakfast, and (c) have at least a passing interest in sex."[1]

If only our interest in sex were a trifle more passing!

Actually, our culture swings between schizo extremes when it comes to this subject. Sex is seen as a rather casual connection between two consenting adults who should be able to partake whenever conversation is a bit lagging. Or sex is so monumentally important that no man and woman deeply in love could survive in the chains of a celibate relationship.

Just where *does* sex figure in to the overall picture of the way men and women relate to each other?

SEX AND THE BIG PICTURE

Our daughter came home recently from one of those free-for-all discussions in a class where everybody contributes their personal opinion at will. Before long, sex and abortion and AIDS occupied center stage. Allison let most of the discussion go by this time until the end, when she offered a few innocuous comments.

Thinking about how much pain can be traced to stepping over sexual boundaries, Allison said, "You know, it seems like our generation would suffer a lot less if premarital sex weren't such a big part of the scene." Simple enough comment.

"Oh, Allison, dry up. You should have lived a hundred years ago."

Ever heard a response like that to something you said? It's sad that the truth spoken in our day and time can bring such ridicule for ideas that have been accepted facts for most of human history. Mark it carefully: conventional morality that said "no" to sex outside of marriage wasn't ascribed to because people were too dumb to know better. It's all part of a much bigger picture.

Sex, from a Christian worldview, is the expression of a total encounter with someone to whom you are committed before God for life—an encounter of mind, body, and spirit. That's why the King James Version of the Bible refers to sex with that wonderful verb, "to know." "Adam knew his wife Eve; and she conceived" (Genesis 4:1). It marks an ending and a new beginning as a couple leaves their family-of-origin to begin one of their own. "For this cause a man shall leave his father and his mother, and shall cleave to his wife; and they shall become one flesh" (Genesis 2:24, NASB). The word *cleave* denotes the idea of "clinging to," a meshing of one's total personality with another person.

Now it's not like Christians don't enjoy the process! C. S. Lewis once noted that pleasure is God's invention, not the devil's.[2] When Abraham's wife, Sarah, heard that she was going to have a child even though she and her husband were quite old, listen to her response. "After I am worn out and my master is old, will I now have this *pleasure*?" (Genesis 18:12, emphasis added). Don't ask us for statistical proof, but we'd wager that the pleasure two people experience who've only known each other sexually would make Casanova blush.

To get the whole picture, you also have to understand what a unique value Christianity places on the physical body. Early Greek philosophy and even later Christian heresy (Gnosticism) held the belief that the physical world (including our bodies) was inherently evil and of little worth compared to the soul and spirit. Christianity said, "No way, José!" (Ever wonder why so many hospitals and medical efforts were founded by Christians?) The body, far from being evil, would one day be reunited with the soul and spirit, to live on in a resurrected state. As a result, while the Romans burned their dead, Christians buried theirs.

Consider the impact this passage must have had on people who, like many moderns, treated the body and its members casually.

> The body is not meant for sexual immorality, but for the Lord, and the Lord for the body. . . . Flee from sexual immorality. All other sins a man commits are outside his body, but he who sins sexually sins against his own body. Do you not know that your body is a temple of the Holy Spirit, who is in you, whom you have received from God? You are not your own; you were bought at a price. Therefore honor God with your body. (1 Corinthians 6:13,18-20)

When Christ died, He redeemed our souls and one day He'll redeem our bodies and give us new ones. *What each of us does with our body is important.* And because sex is a picture of Christ's union with His bride, the Church, sex means something too.

THE COUNTERFEIT

Sir Rabindranath Tagore once said, "I have on my table a violin string. It is free. I twist one end of it and it responds. It is free. But it is not free to do what a violin string is supposed to do — to produce music. So I take it, fix it in my violin and tighten it until it is taut. Only then is it free to be a violin string."[3] Like the violin string that performs its intended function, sexual pleasure produces its sweetest music within the limits of married love.

We know that God always places freedom within a protective fence.

Inside those boundaries there are countless possibilities for innovation. Outside lie chaos and perversion. "It is God's will that you should be sanctified; that you should avoid sexual immorality" (1 Thessalonians 4:3). God's intention in placing the fence around sex is not to smother pleasure, but to provide and protect it for us.

It is common, even among some Christians, to assert that premarital sex is understandable, even permissible, when a couple plans to get married — as though once the elements of love and commitment are injected, the rules change. But there are no conditional clauses attached to the scriptural injunction to "avoid sexual immorality" or to "let the marriage bed be undefiled." The repercussions of experiencing sex before marriage are the same whether a couple plans to marry or not.

There are some lyrics to an old song that express a lie every generation likes to pretend is true. Diana Ross used to sing, "Touch me in the morning, then just walk

away. We don't have tomorrow, but we had yesterday."
That's the problem with sex outside of marriage—you
can't just walk away. We aren't wired together to experience a sexual relationship and then be able to walk away
as though we'd unplugged our mind and emotions.

The act of a moment has far-reaching effects on your
relationship with God, your own personality, and your
relationship to each other.

YOUR RELATIONSHIP TO GOD

"I urge you, as aliens and strangers in the world, to abstain
from sinful desires, which war against your soul" (1 Peter
2:11). Sensuality is contrary to the health of your soul. If
you allow your physical drive to dominate or give a foothold
to immorality, you will feel your walk with God slip into
neutral.

Guilt is a real drag on the spiritual life. Have you noticed
that? And sexual involvement breeds guilt, because there
are boundaries being crossed that each of us knows somehow should be in place. Either a couple has to do some
fancy mental gymnastics to convince themselves that what
they're doing is okay—and they know it isn't really—or
they live with an undertow in the relationship that chips
away the foundation of trust. And they undercut their own
relationship with the Lord.

That's why Paul writes Timothy on this subject with
such clear words: "Flee from youthful lusts, and pursue
after righteousness, faith, love and peace with those who
call on the Lord from a pure heart" (2 Timothy 2:22, NASB).
He says you can't focus your energy in two such intense
directions; you must choose. Let righteousness, faith, love,
and peace occupy you and run in the opposite direction
from the lusts that would carry you out to sea.

YOUR PERSONALITY

Recently, I was counseling a young man in his twenties who was deeply depressed at the loss of a girlfriend he'd been seeing for months. This woman was the one he'd been searching for, he just knew it. And now that she was gone, he was at a loss as to how to pick up his life and go on.

I gathered that sex was just part of the relationship in his mind, like carrying on a lively conversation. He was not a believer, nor did he have much background that would have pointed him in that direction. But I had to ask the question anyway. "Have you ever considered," I asked, "what it would be like to be deeply in love with a woman and not have a sexual relationship with her?"

He really thought about that question—hard. After a few long moments, he said quite honestly, "No, I don't guess I've ever thought about love that wasn't also expressed sexually."

We went on to talk about how that was part of his grief in losing this woman. He had been bonded to her—and sex is a big part of what made that bond soul-deep. The grief he was feeling was very real.

"There is no possibility of having sexual intercourse," wrote Dr. Mary Calderone in a book about sexuality in the family, "without meshing a part of your non-physical self. Sex is such a definite experience that a part of each of you remains forever a part of the other."[4] Given that investment, the question is how often is a person willing to give a part of his or her total self and accept such from someone else with no assurance the investment is for keeps? Parting, in such cases, is *not* such sweet sorrow. It's pain and agony.

"A man who commits adultery lacks judgment; whoever does so *destroys himself*" (Proverbs 6:32, emphasis added). In some profound way, our body and our personal sense of worth are joined. When we share intimately with another, we give away part of our dignity (our God-given sense of nobility and honor). When we don't receive something lasting and meaningful in return, we sense that our dignity has been squandered. In a very real sense, we feel we've lost part of ourselves.

YOUR RELATIONSHIP TO EACH OTHER

Inside a marriage, sex is the most intimate seal of commitment, a tender expression of total giving that binds two people together. Outside of marriage, a focus on the physical has the opposite effect. Sex becomes a wedge, a stumbling block, a hindrance to the development of mature love. What was meant to add life and beauty to a relationship actually undermines its very viability in the long run, for several reasons.

Sex prevents other aspects of the relationship from developing. Although the physical is the most direct route of communication and the easiest to learn, it is only the tip of the iceberg of a good relationship. Anybody can kiss, but not everyone can carry on a real conversation. Often a relationship begun on a plane of physical attraction is never able to reach the deeper intimacy of the mind and the spirit.

Sensuality also hinders sensitivity. It becomes too easy to solve conflicts with a kiss or a hug, or more—rather than develop the ability to talk and pray about them. In marriage, that habit is like putting a bandage on a broken bone, leaving bitter wounds to fester, perhaps never to heal.

The qualities that hold a relationship together—trust, honesty, openness, deep friendship, spiritual intimacy— take time and effort to develop. When you focus on the physical aspect, you short-circuit that process. Physical intimacy is a mistaken attempt to quickly build emotional bridges, but relationships built on such an inadequate foundation eventually collapse. Physical attraction is simply insufficient glue with which to build or maintain a lasting relationship.

Sex injects fear and guilt into the relationship. Premarital intimacy produces guilt feelings because God has wired us together in such a way that we know when we've violated His intentions. "Marriage should be honored by all, and the marriage bed kept pure, for God will judge the adulterer and all the sexually immoral" (Hebrews 13:4). Whether an offender acknowledges God's laws or not, he feels guilty because he is guilty before a holy God.

Do you remember Pavlov's dog—that famous dog that learned to associate a bell with food? Whenever he heard it ring, he began to salivate in anticipation of a meal. Premarital sex often produces an association between guilt, remorse, fear (of pregnancy or being "found out"), and physical intimacy. This cycle of unhealthy feelings, taken into the context of marriage, is a major contributor to frigidity, impotence, and sexual problems.

Sex lays a foundation of distrust and lack of respect. One single woman we know was complaining recently about the meat-market mentality that existed today in some singles' social circles. She said that there are men who calculate the number of dates they must invest with the same woman in order to be confident of having sex. The going figure, it seems, is four dates at about $50 a night, or about $200 for a sexual experience.

How does that make you feel? we asked her. "As though I can be bought—almost like hiring the services of a prostitute," she replied. We offer this example-in-the-extreme to illustrate the way that sex outside of marriage lowers the quotient of *trust* that must be present in a real relationship. Sex without the commitment to the responsibility of marriage and family is just a pleasurable form of using someone. And that's what one or both parties, sooner or later will feel—*used*.

Experiencing intimacy and closeness with someone—without also crossing sexual boundaries—takes a good deal of self-control. Self-control, as you probably remember, is one of the fruits of the Spirit. God gives self-control. And what that means to a relationship is enormous. Self-control actually carves out the space where trust can begin to grow.

Sex causes you to compare one person with others. One young husband admitted that his relationship with his new wife wasn't what he had hoped it would be. "It's really my fault," he admitted. "Before we were married I slept with a number of the girls I dated. Now whenever I kiss my wife or we make love, my memory reminds me that this girl could kiss better than my wife, that girl was better at something else, and so forth. I can't concentrate on loving my wife with all that I am—there have been too many other women in my life to be completely committed to one."

Sex before marriage does increase the likelihood for extramarital sex, studies have shown. If the boundary is crossed before marriage, it's harder to draw a firm line once you're married.

Sex deceives you into thinking you're in love. Studies show that a relationship—any relationship—based on physical attraction may hold itself together for three to five years. During that length of time two people are fooled into thinking, "Well, we've been going together for so long, surely we can make it for a lifetime. This must be love." On the other side of marriage, they wake up to see they had little in common and no basis for a quality relationship.

If what you're feeling is mostly infatuation, it will leave as quickly as it came upon you. Real love stands the test of time; it's strong enough to stand alone without the support of physical intimacy. If you establish a mutually satisfying sexual relationship, you lose objectivity and cheat on the test of time. The only way to rationally decide whether your love is for keeps is to remove any preoccupation with *eros*, sexual love. Otherwise you may marry a mirage, not a person you really know. Sex can blind you.

"ONLY YOU"

Paula and I have been married over twenty years now. And in this day of easy divorce, that seems to mean something. More and more people say, with an air of incredulity, "Really, you've been married to the same person for almost a quarter of a century . . . how have you managed to do that?"

I have to chuckle sometimes when I hear that. I think of all the good times we've shared and it seems that the years have flown by so fast. And I also remember the places in our relationship where we've struggled like any other couple—either colliding in midstream or keeping a wary distance like two big ships who pass silently in the night. Given human nature, this thing of sharing a lifetime with one person is indeed an amazing feat for anyone.

But as I reflect over the years, I see that sex is more important than I even realized. That may sound strange to hear a married couple say, but it's true. Sex is the place where a couple bonds, where they participate in the drama of the most intimate connection of their lives. What I'm saying is that *exclusivity is part of the magic*. That's the way God designed it. The two of us share a connection, an intimate knowledge of the other, that by the grace of God we have shared with no one else on the planet. When hard times come, as they do for any couple, we return to the reality of that deep soul bonding. We are a couple, plain and simple. To separate, to break that bond in some lasting way, would be about as painful as ripping an arm off without anesthesia.

Sex is crucial to the mysterious process of bonding in a lifelong attachment of intimacy. Notice how Paul spoke of the way a man leaves his father and mother and cleaves to his wife and the two enjoy a one-flesh relationship. His very next words are, "This is a profound mystery . . ." (Ephesians 5:32). In other words, this reality defies explanation. Something takes place in the sexual relationship that is far more significant than the act itself. Again, that's the way God designed it. When we have sex outside of marriage, we do not change that reality one bit. *We only undermine our own ability to bond deeply with the one we were meant to live out our days with.* It's like squeezing the glue out of the tube prematurely—there may not be enough left to keep together what needs to be bonded. We have given little pieces of our soul away over the years—scattered them here and there in a way that is very difficult to regather and present to the person we want to love for a lifetime. Only the Spirit of God can restore us enough to let us give ourselves away in a real and holy way again.

If you have already experienced sex outside of marriage, we'd like to share with you how you can begin again, by the grace of God. And if you've read this chapter as a virgin, wondering if there is a solid enough case to postpone sex until marriage, we hope you are convinced. Prize your virginity. Hold on to it like it was worth a million dollars, because it is.

The next time someone even *hints* that being a virgin is being a prude, do something very kind for you both. Chuckle and shake your head. You know better—and some day that individual will, too.

Notes
1. Hornell Hart, as quoted in *Sex, Love, or Infatuation*, by Ray E. Short (Minneapolis, Minn.: Augsburg Publishing House, 1978), p. 45.

2. C. S. Lewis as quoted in *Eros Defiled: The Christian and Sexual Sin*, by John White (Downers Grove, Ill.: InterVarsity Press, 1977), p. 10.
3. Sir Rabindranath Tagore, *Leadership*, Winter 1980, vol. 1, no. 1, p. 117.
4. Mary Calderone and Eric W. Johnson, *The Family Book about Sexuality* (New York: Harper & Row, Publishers, 1979).

Questions for Personal Study and Application

1. Read Genesis 2:18-24. What is God's attitude toward and purpose for sex?
2. Read 1 Corinthians 6:12-20.
   a. What is the relationship between a Christian's body and the Lord?
   b. Why is a Christian to flee from immorality?
3. According to these verses, what effect does following our lusts have on our relationship to God: Psalm 66:18, Isaiah 59:2, Ephesians 5:5-6, Hebrews 13:4?
4. How would you apply those verses personally?
5. According to Proverbs 5:3-6 and 6:32, what are some results of premarital or extramarital sex?
6. Read Romans 13:14, Ephesians 5:3, 2 Timothy 2:22, 1 Peter 1:14, and 4:1-2. How should a believer respond to lust or tempting immorality?
7. David's sin with Bathsheba gives us helpful insight into the predicament of extramarital sex. Read 2 Samuel 11–12 and Psalm 51. What do you learn about the nature of sexual sin, its repercussions, and what it means to experience God's grace?
8. What is the most important application concerning sexual purity that you can make in your life right now?

Suggested Scripture Memory

Ephesians 5:3

Questions for Discussion

1. What kinds of attitudes toward sex do you observe among your friends and acquaintanccs?
2. Read 1 Thessalonians 4:3-5. How would you define the

word *immorality* as used in this passage? Read verses 6-8 as well. Why has God called us? How does this passage apply to dating?

3. How would you define lust? What can it be directed toward in addition to sex?

4. What are some general or specific ways to overcome lust, whatever its object?

5. Two more passages to read are Proverbs 2:16-19 and 9:13-18. What are some of the negative results that come from extramarital sex? How do they compare with the passages from Proverbs? What are some traits of men and women who engage in premarital or extramarital sex?

6. Read Romans 13:14 and 2 Timothy 2:22. What does it mean to "flee from youthful lusts" or to "clothe yourself with Christ"?

CHAPTER SIX

Celibacy in a Sexy World

⊙ ⊙ ⊙

Mike sat quietly in the first group Bible study he'd ever been a part of, hoping that his fidgeting wouldn't be noticed. This was his seventh week and no one had mentioned the thing on his mind — sex. In his mid-thirties, he had been a Christian now for six months and he'd heard a rumor he was starting to believe was true — that Christians held to the idea that sex was meant to be experienced inside marriage. He just couldn't figure it out. How did these people exist without sex? He quizzed his friends, "Look, I just don't understand why sex is not okay; it's an expression of love and caring. What is the deal?" He'd even started looking up every passage under the word *sex* in the concordance of his Bible. "Sex has to be in here somewhere," he reasoned.

Now three years after becoming a Christian, Mike has come a long way. "The first six months were really hard," he admits. "Once I understood what sex *meant*, I thought, *Well, okay, marriage is where sex belongs.* But that still left me with a whole lifestyle to change. Sex was my regular dose of knowing that somebody really liked me. For many reasons, sex was hard to give up."

HARNESSING YOUR SEXUAL DESIRES

How do you feel when you hear words like *self-control* and *celibacy*? Or the perfectly good, but slightly antiquated one, *chastity*? In those words, some people see the caricature of an army sergeant, whistle in hand, demanding compliance with his orders. It's just a big turn-off.

Others see the idea of self-control as something closer to a trapeze artist who submits to the rigors of his craft and learns how to hang with the exquisite tension required to connect — precisely, beautifully, in just the right manner — with the person flying toward him. The very quality that incubates such artistry is his self-control. Self-control — which is necessary for living well and for living celibate — is not a negative thing.

When the Bible speaks of self-control, especially in sexual matters, the connotations are always positive. God is not a drill sergeant ready to slap a few wrists at the first sign that anybody's having fun on the job. Self-control has a purpose — and that purpose is positive. Let your mind ponder these verses:

> Each of you should learn to control his own body in a way that is holy and honorable, not in passionate lust like the heathen, who do not know God. (1 Thessalonians 4:4-5)

> But I discipline my body and bring it into subjection, lest when I have preached to others, I myself should be disqualified. (1 Corinthians 9:27, NKJV)

> But the fruit of the Spirit is love, joy, peace, kindness, goodness, faithfulness, gentleness, patience, and *self-control*. (Galatians 5:22, emphasis added)

Self-control, or the ability to make an active choice about where I direct the energies of my body and soul, is the gateway virtue to a host of others. The implication of these passages is that if we can harness and direct, by God's grace, our own sexual drive—then we can subdue other powerful forces in our lives. Self-control opens the door to the ability to invest our energies in other vital ways to connect with others. If we live as the slave of our own urges— we will never gather the courage and fortitude required to love others well.

John White, in his book on sexuality, *Eros Defiled*, explains that living celibately could be called an experience of "sexual fasting." He compares sexual fasting to abstinence from food. It only works well, he claims, if we view it as something we actively choose.

> Starving people can be in one of two states. Some experience hunger as torture. They fight, steal, even kill to get food. Others experience no hunger at all.
>
> It depends upon the attitude (or mindset) of the starving person. If, for instance, I decide voluntarily to fast, I will experience hunger for a couple of days and then suddenly a strange absence of hunger. If, on the other hand, I have no wish to fast and you deprive me of food, I will spend my days drooling over visions of it and my nights dreaming about it. My hunger will grow intolerable.[1]

In other words, it's crucial that you or I think of purity as something that we choose. Self-control grows out of a perspective that sees sexuality as good and God-given and expressed in a hundred ways that don't culminate in intercourse. To exercise restraint, then, is to take that God-given energy and redirect it elsewhere.

Sexual energy can be sublimated in other powerful and creative avenues. That's why author Luci Swindoll, a woman who remained single, wrote a book on singleness and sexuality in which she claimed that though her bed was narrow—her world was wide. She transformed the limitations of her sexual options into an array of many others—travel, close friendships, impact in her career, depth in her walk with God.

The principle of sublimation has long been accepted on a larger societal scale. J. D. Unwin, a respected Cambridge University sociologist, found in his study of over eighty ancient, primitive and even more modern societies that there was an unvarying correlation between the degree of sexual restraints and the rate of social progress. "Cultures that were more sexually permissive displayed less cultural energy, creativity, intellectual development, individualism, and a slower general cultural ascent."[2]

Arnold Toynbee, the renowned student of world history, believed that a culture that postpones sexual experience in young adults is more prone to progress. In their lifelong research project, *The Story of Civilization*, the late Will and Ariel Durant declare that sex in the young "is a river of fire that must be banked and cooled by a hundred restraints if it is not to consume in chaos both the individual and the group."[3]

So a lifestyle of purity, or postponing sexual experience, can open up easily as many possibilities as it curtails. It's really a question of mindset. Do we see exercising sexual self-control as a giant pain that represents the clipping of our wings? Or is it something difficult, maybe—but nevertheless something that leads us in a good and life-giving direction?

If sexual self-control is a "no" that leads to many more and better "yeses" down the road, then it will seem like a *choice*—a choice that each of us is indeed capable of making in the grace of God.

A MINDSET THAT PROMOTES PURITY

A lifestyle of purity begins in the mind. It doesn't just *happen*. Our culture is too sensual and the opportunities for immorality are so plentiful, that developing a lifestyle of purity is a conscious choice, for most of us, married or single. It requires a change of thinking—and a change of heart. One guy made an interesting observation about this process in himself. He said, "I used to think that the more I did (sexually) with a girl, the more it meant she liked me." Change meant for him a whole new orientation to the way he equated something sexual to love. There are two primary mental bridges to cross en route to a lifestyle of purity.

PURITY IS POSSIBLE

The subliminal message these days is that any normal person with any normal range of hormones will, of course, be sexually active. How could they not be? And if, for some reason, they aren't, then it's because they aren't "normal." As Rosalie de Rosset writes,

> There is little praise for the consistently sexually controlled single. Too often, it is mixed with granulated pity or powdered condescension. Ironically, while discipline and self-control are encouraged and admired in scholarship, athletics, music and ministry, their absence is strangely excused in sexual matters. The secular myth has infiltrated the Christian consciousness that our sexual urges are overpowering and irresistible. There will come the moment when we "simply can't help ourselves," when "madness" will

overtake us, when "it will be bigger than us." To resist the madness is somehow a failure to comprehend true sexuality, to be pronounced neuter—if not audibly, then certainly subconsciously.[4]

The internal obstacle we have to overcome is that of seeing a sexually pure life as a true possibility and one that denotes strength and character, rather than deficiency.

When you think of how overstimulated our culture is sensually, it's helpful to remember that we are not the first people to live in such a climate. It's entirely possible that the people in Corinth that Paul wrote to had it worse. Corinth was the sensual Disneyland of its day. The center of attraction in Corinth was the worship of Aphrodite in a huge temple erected in her honor. If you had lived in Corinth, you would have been subject to the practice of "conscription." Young men and women were drafted into the role of being temple prostitutes. Sex and worship, two powerful human needs, were combined into one hedonistic act.

Knowing this background adds significant comfort and encouragement to Paul's words from 1 Corinthians 10:13— "No temptation has seized you except what is common to man. And God is faithful; he will not let you be tempted beyond what you can bear. But when you are tempted, he will also provide a way out so that you can stand up under it."

Paul wrote those words to people who actually had worship confused with sex! If there were ways to overcome temptation successfully in their day—it's possible in ours.

PURITY IS NEEDED
The second mental obstacle is that of being willing to take the steps necessary to let a lifestyle of purity take root as a way of life.

RESIST THE BEGINNINGS

Individuals and couples who decide to maintain high standards in their relationships know that it is easier not to start a car than it is to put it in reverse. Let us explain.

Fruit salesmen sometimes frequent our neighborhood with fresh truckloads from California. But since we know we can buy the same fruit cheaper at the grocery store, we usually decline politely soon after we open the door.

However, on one notable occasion, the salesman was able to overcome our resistance rather quickly. His method? As soon as Paula opened the door, he held out an orange slice and said, "Wouldn't you like to taste this California orange?" She consented and before long, she was following him down to his truck, checkbook in hand. She came home with a whole box of oranges — expensive oranges — from California!

It's much the same scenario in matters that are sexual in nature. Few of us have enough self-control to be able to taste sensual pleasure to any degree and turn back. Just like my wife, we find ourselves buying fruit we never intended to.

It's easier in the long run to establish standards in your relationships that keep you from starting what you can't, in good faith, finish. As the Song of Songs says, "Do not stir up nor awaken my love until she pleases" (3:5, NASB). That's a poetic Hebrew way of saying, "Don't begin what you can't complete." Don't walk so close to the edge that you never know when you might fall off.

Immorality, in any real sense, begins not in an act — but in the thoughts we allow ourselves to entertain. That can be a difficult concept to buy — after all, who cares (and who will ever know) what you think about? Jesus said that as a man thinks in his heart, so he is (Matthew 12:34). And that is so true. What we give mental space to in a serious way—we will eventually act out. That's why the real beginnings of immorality, in any sense, are in our mental life.

It's one thing to notice a beautiful woman, an attractive guy; it's quite another to allow lust to take hold. (The old expression is that you may notice the birds flying overhead, but you don't have to allow one to build a nest in your hat.) Mental immorality—mental adultery—is where the real battle must be fought and won. If you struggle with significant problems in your thought life, you may want to consider the state of your relationships in general. Preoccupation with sensuality is often a signal that our actual relationships are so shallow or so nonexistent that we are using a fantasy life of some sort to fill the void.

ESTABLISH YOUR OWN CONVICTIONS

Perhaps you've wished that someone would spell out the limits of physical contact. "It's okay to do this, but going this far is too far." When the lights were turned low and the music got soft, though, what would you do then? Relying on someone else's opinion would give little strength and comfort.

If you establish your own convictions as something you've thought and prayed over, you won't ignore your own conscience quite so easily. To come up with your own standards, you have to be honest with yourself about what's a turn-on and what's not. You must set limits for yourself—and be prepared to respect those limits for someone else.

When we asked singles, "How are you able to live chastely with the opposite sex, in a culture like ours?" over and over we got this response: "I have to know my own limits, and I have to talk about that openly." They agreed that it helps if both the guy and the girl are gatekeepers. Sometimes they followed suggestions others had handed down to them—like don't be out after midnight, stay vertical and don't get horizontal, keep your feet on the floor, etc. But the common element was always that of knowing—and communicating—your limits. Some of the ways they did that were rather creative: "I know myself and this is the limit I've set for my own sanity. . . ." Or, "I find you really attractive, so is it okay with you if I don't kiss you? I'd really like to get to know you better."

Putting something about your limits into words seems to be important, for a number of reasons. First, it gets the hidden out in the open and makes it seem real. And then putting words to your limits keeps the other person from thinking they're "some kind of hideous beast." It takes the pressure off.

Remember that we are each "wired" in such a way as to know intuitively that physical intimacy should lead to intercourse. Physical intimacy is *meant* to lead to intercourse. "Starting and stopping" is not what our sexual computers are programmed for. And similarly, God did not design us to continually engage in physical intimacy that leaves us unsatisfied. Some call this the "domino theory of love." With each contact, your desire accelerates but the thrill of that particular activity decreases. So if you really enjoyed kissing him last time, you're going to want more than that the next time.

PREVENTIVE THERAPY

Many a pastor has sat through a counseling appointment with a nervous couple contemplating marriage. As the story unfolds, the couple has been dating for some time. They seem very much in love—or sometimes they just think they are and they've wanted time to be sure.

"So why are you thinking about marriage now?" the question is put to them. And the answer which emerges is that somehow—even though they hadn't meant to—they got sexually involved. Perhaps, now, they ought to just go ahead and get married.

Many, many couples have ended up in bed together—who never intended that to happen.

How can the best of intentions go awry? Often, it's the most basic of principles in relationships that have been overlooked. For instance, a couple may neglect to talk very openly about the natural chemistry between them and how they're going to avoid compromising situations.

Talking about the kind of standards you want to keep is a type of preventive therapy for immorality.

Another important principle is the need to *avoid situations* where you will be alone together without the potential for interruption. In this day of open visitation in college dorms and apartments, that may take some planning. But planning is basic to a good relationship. The premium needs to be placed on activity and conversation. Communication is the art you will spend most of your life refining. Being in places where no one else is can spell disaster.

When we understand how strong the pull toward the sensual aspect of a relationship really is, Paul's words make such sense. "Flee from youthful lusts," he wrote, and "pursue after righteousness, faith, love and peace" (2 Timothy 2:22, NASB). Don't assume you are stronger than the temptation. Flee! Acknowledge how hard the struggle is and run away—and then run toward those things that will build the character and spiritual depth in your life you long for.

REGAINING LOST VIRGINITY

We have a friend who, for nearly ten years, has toured the country speaking to college groups. One of the big topics, as you might imagine, is male-female relationships. She stresses the importance of virginity and what it means to a relationship in the long run. She talks about the difference that knowing Christ makes in the whole picture.

"Every time I give this talk," she says, "I can count on a steady stream of people afterwards asking how they can undo what they've done. They want to know how they can experience forgiveness and start over, after they have already experienced a sexual relationship with someone."

Certainly, large numbers of sexually active singles bear out her experience. Many people lose their virginity before they are far enough along in life to even know what they lost. Or before they understand that it is possible to come back from the experience.

When Andy was a senior in high school, he began to attend a Bible study for kids his age after school. He also began to get seriously interested in a girl named Kimberly. Every weekend they were together. And while they both knew that sex before marriage was wrong, they ended up sleeping together before the year was out. Andy felt he had committed the unforgivable sin. He tried and tried to pull back, to spend time with Kim without sex. And every time, he failed. He felt all alone in the struggle. There was no one he could tell that he could be confident would help without condemning him.

He slowly concluded that the Christian life was impossible and pulled away altogether.

If you're reading this book and your virginity is past tense, we want to address this next section to you. It's not possible to rewrite your story or technically restore your virginity, but by the grace of God you can experience a fresh new beginning in your life—a restoration of innocence and hope. Paul said that the goal of all we learned about the Lord is "love, which comes from a pure heart and *a good conscience* and a sincere faith" (1 Timothy 1:5, emphasis added).

It's encouraging to realize that there is no sin you or I have committed that's beyond God's forgiveness. Three of the women mentioned in Christ's genealogy (Matthew 1:1-16) were involved in overt sin. They were socially unacceptable, yet God chose to include these women in the genealogy of Christ. God is in the business of forgiving and transforming sinners, a group that includes us all.

"As far as the east is from the west, so far has he removed our transgressions from us" (Psalm 103:12). "I, even I, am he who blots out your transgressions, for my own sake, and remembers your sins no more" (Isaiah 43:25). When you experience God's forgiveness, you are given a new lease on life and relationships.

Or consider this incredible passage from Hebrews. "The blood of goats and bulls and the ashes of a heifer sprinkled on those who are ceremonially unclean sanctify them so that they are outwardly clean. How much more, then, will the blood of Christ, who through the eternal Spirit offered himself unblemished to God, cleanse our consciences from acts that lead to death, so that we may serve the living God!" (9:13-14).

Sometimes experiencing forgiveness and a clean start is harder than just knowing intellectually that God has forgiven you. May we offer some steps suggested to us by a counselor who has helped many people find their way out of a maze of guilt?

REAL REPENTANCE

Ask God to bring to your mind everything from your past that bothers you presently and that has violated His principles and commands. Make a list of all that comes to your mind. Take the time to pray about everything on your list. "Lord, I really want to turn from my past. I know I did the wrong thing and I want to be free from ever falling prey to these sins again. Father, thank You that the blood of Christ covers my sin, even these sins. Thank You that I can be free of these entanglements."

As you tear up your list and throw it away, continue to thank God for the way that He has bought you back from your past.

You may need to return to the individual or individuals with whom you engaged in sexual sin and ask their forgiveness as well. We cannot be sexually involved with someone without leaving scars that affect them, too.

> As obedient children, do not conform to the evil
> desires you had when you lived in ignorance. For
> you know that it was not with perishable things
> such as silver or gold that you were redeemed from
> the empty way of life handed down to you from your
> forefathers, but with the precious blood of Christ, a
> lamb without blemish or defect. (1 Peter 1:14,18-19)

Begin to immerse yourself in the Scriptures that underscore the reality of God's love and grace and mercy. You cannot build a new beginning out of trying to do better or a litany of "have-to's" and "ought-to's." Only deepening your experience of Christ will give you the grace for a real life change.

REAL TRANSPARENCY

Sexual sin is usually a private matter between two individuals. Breaking free of sexual sin, though, is often helped immensely by bringing the offenses committed out into the open, in the form of sharing with another person. James speaks of this: "Therefore confess your sins to each other and pray for each other so that you may be healed" (James 5:16). While transparency usually involves risk, God often uses another person to mirror His love and acceptance and forgiveness back to us, and in this way, brings healing to many wounds.

REDEMPTIVE SEXUALITY

Whether we're single or married, each of us is charged with the task of contending with our sexuality — and also learning to enjoy our sexuality in healthy, positive ways. If you're still a virgin, take whatever steps are necessary to guard that gift. As the advertisement says so well, "You're worth waiting for." If your innocence and sexual purity is something you long to regain, allow God to restore your body, mind, and soul. He is the ultimate transformer of lives.

The next time you wonder what you're supposed to do with all this sexual energy as a single person, thank God that He created such a wondrous way of communicating His intimacy with us. Thank Him that He used your sexual nature to mirror such profound truth in such a concrete, visceral way. He intends for sexual longing to pull us toward marriage so that we have ample reason to overcome our fears and take the risk to really love someone . . . for a lifetime.

Notes
1. John White, *Eros Defiled: The Christian and Sexual Sin* (Downers Grove, Ill.: InterVarsity, 1978), p. 28.
2. J. D. Unwin, as quoted in "How to Put Premarital Sex on Hold," by Reo M. Christenson, *Christianity Today*, 19 February 1982, p. 17.
3. Will and Ariel Durant, as quoted in "How to Put Premarital Sex on Hold."
4. Rosalie de Rosset, "Chaste by Choice," *Christianity Today*, 19 February 1982, p. 18.

Questions for Study and Personal Application

1. God's will concerning our bodies is very clear for believers. Read 1 Thessalonians 4:3-8.
   a. What are we to do?
   b. What are we not to do?
   c. Based on God's will, what would the dating relationship be like between two believers?
2. Read James 1:13-15. Describe the path to sexual sin.
3. Consider Luke 6:45 and describe how you think a person best goes about changing their thought life. Look up the following verses and jot down some thoughts in answer to this question: Deuteronomy 6:6-7; Joshua 1:8; Psalm 119:9,11; 2 Corinthians 10:5.
4. What environments or activities encourage thoughts that lead you in the wrong direction?
5. How would you personally define purity in a dating relationship? Be as specific as you think you need to be.
6. How does Proverbs 22:3 apply to the activities related to dating?
7. According to 1 John 1:9, what is our responsibility when we become aware of sin in our lives?
8. What does God do with our sin as Christians? Answer this question from the following verses: Psalm 103:12; Isaiah 38:17, 43:25; Micah 7:19.
9. What is your present attitude toward pure dating relationships? In what way, if any, has this study encouraged you to change your attitudes and actions?

Suggested Scripture Memory

1 Thessalonians 4:3

Questions for Discussion

1. What does it mean to defraud someone? What are some ways that men defraud women in a dating relationship? What are some ways that women defraud men? What percentage of your friends, Christian and nonChristian, have immoral physical relationships outside of marriage? What are some reasons why this is so?

3. Can you share an illustration of how God changed your thought life? What helped this process?

4. How can a person's thought life affect his or her actions in a dating relationship?

5. Why should believers pursue purity in dating?

6. Can you share what effect the truth of God's forgiveness has had on your life?

CHAPTER SEVEN

Singleness

ꙮ ꙮ ꙮ

Most small children go through a period where they discover the concept of "mine." "It's mine!" they insist, whatever "it" is. When our son, Brady, was a toddler we developed a little scenario between us, a spin-off of his newly burgeoning concept of "mine."

I would grab an object and say, "Mine. This belongs to me." Then Brady would laugh and snatch it out of my hand and say, "No, mine." Back and forth we would go with this little game until one of us got tired. Then I'd grab Brady and hug him tight. "Brady, you're mine. You belong to me." And his face would absolutely light up with the sheer and total pleasure of being wanted . . . of *belonging* to someone.

Of course, Brady didn't really "belong" to me, nor I to him. But in his face I could recognize the longing undisguised, the universal desire to belong and to feel intensely wanted by another person. We all long to belong. It's this deep primal desire that eventually brings us to the Lord and whatever true moments of rest we've known as believers come from experiencing the most profound reality of the faith: we *belong* to Christ and He has pledged Himself to us. In some amazing grace-filled way, He has embraced us in a big bear hug, right at the core of our being. Can you believe it? We are His!

This longing to belong to someone is an aspect of what brings us into marriage. And it's also part of what can make singleness particularly painful at times. We'd like to explore the whole question of singleness — why the Scripture presents the single state as a viable option, how it can be an unprecedented opportunity . . . and how, sometimes, it can also be a weak escape from the rigors of a long-term relationship.

SINGLENESS AS A VIABLE OPTION

Paul spent his life as a single man serving Jesus Christ and he was hot on the idea. Marriage, in his opinion, was a definite second best. He wasted no energy, it seems, wondering if there was something wrong with him. Singleness presented a rare spiritual opportunity. It was definitely a viable option for a way to invest a life.

> Because of the present distress . . . it is good for a man to remain as he is: Are you bound to a wife? Do not seek to be loosed. Are you loosed from a wife? Do not seek a wife. But even if you do marry, you have not sinned; and if a virgin marries, she has not sinned. Nevertheless such will have trouble in the flesh, but I would spare you. But this I say, brethren, the time is short, so that from now on even those who have wives should be as though they had none, those who weep as though they did not weep, those who rejoice as though they did not rejoice, those who buy as though they did not possess, and those who use this world as not misusing

it. For the form of this world is passing away. But I
want you to be without care. He who is unmarried
cares for the things of the Lord—how he may
please the Lord. (1 Corinthians 7:26-32, NKJV)

Paul had no romantic notions about the day he lived
in—it was difficult, demanding, and hostile to the faith.
You can imagine what he would say about ours! His point
is that if you marry, you must be prepared to contend with
that difficulty and hostility as it comes against your family.
The effect multiplies.

SINGLENESS SIMPLIFIES LIFE

Have you ever watched a couple with two or three small
children in tow as they waited in a crowded airport? Dia-
per bags and strollers and crying babies—it's enough to
make you take up a collection to hire a live-in nanny to
help. Paul is reminding us that it's easier to navigate life as
a single person.

In the *King James Version*, 1 Corinthians 7:28 reads,
"Nevertheless such shall have trouble in the flesh." Those
who study the Greek tell us that the word *flesh* refers to
our lower nature, and the word *trouble* is derived from a
Greek word that means "to press together." If you marry
those two concepts, you realize that in the close proximity
of marriage and family, all that "humanness" rubs up
against each other. Living together well means there's a lot
to sort out and smooth over. Are you willing, for instance,
to invest an evening deciding whose home you'll visit for
Christmas or whether you'll spend your income tax refund
on a camper or a computer? There's a lot of everydayness
that happens inside the walls that house a family.

But the real thrust of Paul's passage on singleness is
that the single state translates into the chance to live a life

focused on the Lord. "Undistracted devotion," Paul calls it. You don't have to be concerned about the host of details and challenges that confront a family.

Listen to the words of a single man as he breaks off a relationship with a woman in order to invest his energy elsewhere:

> There is one thing in which I am dead earnest about and that is the communist cause. It is my life, my business, my religion. It is my hobby, my sweet-heart, my wife, my mistress, my bread, my meat. I work at it in the daytime and I dream of it at night. Its hold on me grows, not lessens, as time goes on. Therefore, I cannot carry on a relationship with you any longer, no longer a love affair, not even a conversation with others without relating it to this force which drives and guides my life. I evaluate books and people and ideas and actions according to how they affect this communist cause and by their attitude toward it. I've already been in jail because of my ideals, and, if necessary, I'm ready to go before a firing squad.[1]

Does that sound like commitment-in-the-extreme? It's merely the words of parting a young communist recruit wrote the woman he loved in order to give himself to the "cause," the Communist Party. There's a radical element to being a Christian, too, and a cause that makes any impassioned political dissident pale in comparison. The gospel is not just good news—it's the pivotal truth of the universe. God became a man and dwelt among us and we've beheld His glory. That's a cause worth the investment of a whole life.

Jim, a friend that Stacy knew well in seminary, was married for about five years—just long enough to complete seminary. Then his wife left, admitting that she had never "bought in" to the whole spiritual thing. Furthermore, she wasn't sure she loved him, either. It was the business world that really captivated her.

Jim did not feel free to remarry. Instead, he decided to invest his life in a part of the world that few Americans are allowed to enter. He has been there ten years now, living a quiet Christian witness in neighborhoods where no one, ever, met a practicing Christian. A steady stream of men who have grown spiritually to the point where they can help others have come from his life. Jim knew that the task before him in a hostile, dangerous environment could be best accomplished as a single man.

SEEING SINGLENESS AS AN OPPORTUNITY

Okay, so it's a real option to stay single. Marriage is not required, no matter how much your married friends hint. Both singleness and marriage have particular limitations, as well as compensations. How do you deal, then, with the feelings and struggles of being single, in day-to-day life? A number of our single friends shared their thoughts with us.

First, they all insist that you must be able to divorce your state (single or married) from your worth. Being single is not about being defective merchandise. Marriage is not a merit badge you earn with enough accumulated spiritual brownie points. God blesses the life of His children—married ones and single ones.

The consensus is that it's terribly important to cultivate a broad span of relationships within the Body of Christ. Old, young, married, single, divorced the more connected you are to others, the more balance you will sense in your life. Developing friendships—especially with other families—often requires some effort. We know single people who offer to help with yard work or care for small children or, in some way, go out of their way to bridge the gap and forge a friendship. It's worth the effort.

Everyone agrees that living in the present is the prescription for sanity. Too many singles postpone life, as though only marriage could give them the permission to buy a home or invest in china. One wrote, "We view our jobs as temporary until a man (or woman) comes along. We remember wistfully or we dream hopefully, but we despair of the present, for there is no man (or woman) in the present."[2] The psalmist reminds us, "This is the day the LORD has made; let us rejoice and be glad in it" (Psalm 118:24). Today is the day to enter wholeheartedly into whatever the business is at hand. Let yourself live in all the joy and possibility of the present.

All of us know what it is to have unfulfilled longings. Many singles report that the desire for companionship, for marriage, comes in seasons, with waves of longing that tend to sweep over them. The psalmist said,

> All my longings lie open before you, O Lord;
>   my sighing is not hidden from you. (Psalm 38:9)

One friend admitted there are times she has really wanted to be married and yet she also appreciates that she has known aspects of God that the average married woman does not know. "I know Him as my Best Friend, my Helper, my Choicest Companion—needs that the Lord commonly meets for a married woman through her husband." The lonely times become an invitation to get closer to Him, remembering that the Lord Himself, often misunderstood and rejected, was single for thirty-three years. "For we do not have a high priest who is unable to sympathize with our weaknesses" (Hebrews 4:15).

SINGLENESS AS AN ESCAPE

There are, as you can see, some very solid reasons for being single, even for staying single. But being single can also be born of fear. It used to be that couples jumped into marriage as the next obvious step in their master life plan. You grew up, went to school, met and married a Christian you found attractive and worked hard to make it work. Now the pendulum has swung in the opposite direction. There are fewer couples jumping into marriage without thinking . . . and more who are waiting and waiting and waiting. There are more people who are staying single . . . but often, not for very good reasons.

We are part of a young and growing congregation near the center of Raleigh. Some of the most interesting singles in town worship with us every week. But recently, Stacy and I noticed a disturbing reality. In the three years we have been part of this congregation, no one has gotten married! "What gives?" I began to ask some of these very singles. "Why have there been no marriages among so many single people?"

Time and again, I heard the same responses. "There's this tendency to just hang out with people until this really perfect individual comes along." Or, "marriage just seems like this huge, terribly risky step to take." And with every year, a few more qualities are added to the list and working out a relationship over time looks more difficult. Until the whole prospect of marriage looks about as feasible as scaling Mount Everest barefooted.

When we probe beneath the fear of commitment and marriage, we discover that many of today's singles are themselves the children of divorce. They know, firsthand, that sometimes "things don't work out." They have experienced firsthand the pain of a family breaking up. Even some of their friends, whose weddings they were in, may not still be together. They're told, "Hey, you better not make the same mistake we did. You better look really hard before you leap."

That advice can get pretty unnerving at times. I think of one single friend deep in the throes of trying to decide whether to marry a guy she'd been seeing seriously for a couple of years. They knew each other well—well enough to know how controlling his mother is and all about her need for more reassurance than he could comfortably give. "I don't know if we can sort all this out on the other side of marriage," she confided near tears as we talked over coffee. "Maybe he will never be able to move toward me like I need without seeing some version of his mother."

I really felt for her. What a puzzle to unravel, with half the pieces missing. It used to be that most dating couples would not have stopped to think about how anybody's mother could influence their relationship. Or if they had, they wouldn't have had a clue. But with all the talk about relationships—and all the divorce statistics—couples can sometimes analyze the life right out of their relationship. *There will always be potential problems when two human beings get together*. There will always be things to work out. Getting married is about saying that you love each other and you are willing to trust God to give the grace to bear the pain involved in living out that love.

Because people are staying single longer, it's possible to continue forever just to sample the smorgasbord of potential relationships. One single guy in his thirties said, "I'm frustrated with women who can't seem to make up their minds. They want to be entertained and taken out— without having to declare more. I get the feeling, sometimes, that I'm just supposed to fill a role so they won't be lonely." Perhaps this is the kind of scene that prompted one writer for singles to title his book *Call It Love Or Call It Quits*.

Good reasons for remaining single exist—but fear of sacrifice or commitment is not one of them. William Willimon, minister of Duke Chapel, speaks of how Christian relationships have always moved past the satin-and-white-lace of the usual wedding with honest words like "for better, for worse, for richer, for poorer, in sickness and in health." He says that as believers, "We have no definition of love (a cross being on our altar) that is sacrifice or risk-free. Relationships between men and women that go beyond merely hanging around take time, hard work, tough mindedness, and a host of other mundane virtues."[3]

If you choose to remain single, let it be because God has led you to prize the opportunities your singleness offers. Don't stay single out of the fear that you might not have what it takes to make a marriage work.

I sometimes think of the scene a friend recently told us about. Two men—one married, one single—peeked around the bedroom door where the married man's four-year-old son lay sleeping, absolutely cherubic in his miniature baseball cap and dirty cheeks. "See that, John?" he said. "That's worth every disappointment and every misunderstanding in a marriage that you will ever experience."

Notes
1. As quoted in *Singleness*, by Charles R. Swindoll (Portland, Oreg.: Multnomah, 1981), p. 22.
2. Judy Douglas, *Old Maid Is a Dirty Word* (San Bernardino, Calif.: Here's Life Publishers, 1979), p. 42.
3. William Willimon, "Risky Business," *Christianity Today*, 19 February 1989.

Questions for Personal Study and Application

1. How do the following verses relate to singleness: Psalm 73:25-26; Jeremiah 29:11; 1 Timothy 6:6?
2. Look up Psalm 139:13-14; Matthew 11:28-29; Luke 12:6-7; and Romans 9:20. What thoughts do you have about God's concern for you and control of your circumstances?
3. From 1 Corinthians 7:1-10, what are some reasons to get married, and what are some reasons to remain single?
4. Read Matthew 19:3-12.
    a. Why did the disciples think it might be better not to marry?
    b. What three reasons for celibacy does Jesus give?
5. What kinds of fears of commitment/marriage do you feel you have?
6. Do you think it is possible to live a fulfilled life as a single person? Why, or why not?

Suggested Scripture Memory

1 Corinthians 7:7

Questions for Discussion

1. What are the lifestyles of some of your Christian acquaintances over thirty who have not yet been married? In what ways do you see application of these verses—or the lack of it—in the attitudes and actions of these people?
2. What are some of modern pressures against not yet being married or planning to remain single? How can the verses listed be helpful in withstanding those pressures?

3. How would you describe "undivided devotion"? Do you know someone who has made a decision to remain single for this purpose? What is his or her life like?
4. What do you think Paul meant in 1 Corinthians 7:7?
5. What do you think Jesus meant in Matthew 19:11?
6. How does your view of your marital status affect the way you view God's plans for your life?

CHAPTER EIGHT

This Is Getting Serious

ꙮ ꙮ ꙮ

How to know when you've met the person you should marry . . . is an ageless question, one that's guaranteed to tie a person's stomach in knots trying to answer at times. Single people make a regular habit of asking their married friends how they knew they'd met the man or woman they could spend a lifetime with. The standard frustrating answer, it seems, is "Oh, don't worry. You'll *know* when you've met the right one. You'll just know it." Some enchanted evening you'll look across a crowded room and there she'll be, the woman of your dreams.

Does that sound like a fairy tale . . . or a line from *South Pacific*, maybe? Oh, that it were so easy to discern! Truthfully, there is a feeling of *rightness* about a good relationship, the sense that the two of us are a good fit. Often a couple can report with some confidence, "We know that God led us to be together." But there are plenty of couples with great marriages who will tell you they took that big step with hefty doses of faith and courage. I know of at least one woman, the mother of four and happily married for twenty-four years, who prayed all the way down the aisle that God would strike her dead if she was making a mistake! We don't recommend that degree of anxiety to anyone. Basically, the old maxim that's never been improved upon is "first you labor to make the right choice (in a marriage partner) and then you work to make the choice right."

It would be convenient if we could settle the question with the same confidence that Abraham's servant had when he set out to find a bride for Isaac. "Oh LORD . . . may it be that when I say to a girl, 'Please let down your jar that I may have a drink,' and she says, 'Drink, and I'll water your camels too'—let her be the one you have chosen for your servant Isaac" (Genesis 24:12-14). When a lovely girl named Rebekah responded in such a fashion, Abraham's servant knew his mission was accomplished.

Unfortunately, we know of no twentieth century enactment of this joining of two lives. Each of us, it seems, must settle with God whether a relationship is getting serious—and whether marriage is the next obvious step. You are the one who must answer whether you've met someone you could spend a lifetime getting to know. Whose little annoying habits can you endure, whose infinite possibilities do you want to explore? Whose soggy, wadded-up washcloth do you want to hang up daily? Whose weaknesses are you willing to tolerate, and whose joys and sorrows are you anxious to share? Whatever your response, there will always be an element of courage required of you. (Remember there are no guarantees in relationships . . . not the real ones, anyway.) Marriage is a step of faith.

HOW WILL YOU RECOGNIZE REAL LOVE?

Possibly you are wondering as you read this book whether a current dating relationship, or perhaps a past one, constitutes real love and is a relationship you should pursue.

You want to know, and rightly so, whether or not the twitch-iness in your stomach is indicative of a love that endures or just starry-eyed infatuation. As you reflect on this, consider the differences between real love and what seems to be love.

REAL LOVE IS KNOWLEDGEABLE

If what you are feeling for another person is love, then that feeling will be based on having seen the other person in many situations over a period of time. Love deepens as knowledge of the other person grows and many aspects of his or her personality attract you. Ask yourself, How many characteristics of this person can I list, and what proof do I have to substantiate those traits?

On the other hand, if what you're feeling is infatuation, the number of factors that attract you to him or her is rel-atively few. You're bewitched by her blue eyes or enamored of his athletic ability, but how about his or her lifestyle and goals? Is it an affinity for pizza and movies that binds you together, or a shared outlook on life?

When two people are infatuated, they live in a roman-tic fantasyland. Whether they've known each other for a few months or even a number of years, faults and weaknesses are hidden behind a superficial guise. Each person loves the image he or she has created of the other.

Dr. James Peterson summarizes the characteristics of infatuated love (which he refers to as romance):

First, romance results in such distortions of person-ality that after marriage the two people can never fulfill the roles that they expect of the other. Second, romance so idealizes marriage and even sex that when the day-to day experiences of marriage are encountered, there must be disillusionment involved. Third, the romantic complex is so shortsighted that the premarital relationship is conducted almost entirely on the emotional level and consequently, such problems as temperamental or value differences, religious or cultural differences, financial, occupational, or health problems are never considered. Fourth, romance develops such a false ecstasy that there is implied in courtship promise of a kind of happiness which could never be maintained during the realities of married life. Fifth, romance is such an escape from the negative aspects of personality to the extent that their repression obscures the real person.[1]

A person who experiences real love is not afraid to admit his own shortcomings, or those of the other person. Could you say, "I am fully aware of your temper, and I love you in spite of your short fuse"? While it is true that you usually have a somewhat idealized conception of the person you love, nevertheless there must be a total willingness to check that perception with reality and accept what you see.

The foundation of love upon which you build a lifetime relationship must be knowledgeable, unconditional commitment to the one you marry. As Maxine Hancock writes, "It's knowing that you and she will still care about each other when sex and day dreams, fights, and futures—when all that's on the shelf and done with. Love—well I'll tell you what love is: It's you at seventy-five and her at seventy-one, each of you listening for the other's step in the next room, each afraid that sudden silence, a sudden cry, could mean a lifetime's talk is over."[2]

REAL LOVE IS A RESPONSE TO THE TOTAL PERSON
Of the three Greek words for love—*eros, phileo*, and *agape*—infatuation consists almost exclusively of the first

two, eros and phileo. Eros is a sensual, sexual expression of love that seeks to enjoy and possess the object of affection.

The response is more to a body and a face than a total person, complete with mind, emotions, and personality. If the element of physical communication is removed from the relationship, there is often little attraction left. It is commonly associated with the phrase, "I love you if you do such and such to please me."

Phileo is that variety of rapport we call "brotherly love," a type of mutual appreciation where both people benefit from a relationship of shared interests. "I love you because" (of some particular trait) is the phrase often used to illustrate phileo love.

Agape love is an unconditional response to the total person: "I love you in spite of" (the weaknesses I see in you). Any relationship that endures must possess this level of concern for the welfare of someone without any desire to control that person, to be thanked by him, or to enjoy the process. It reaches beyond to a "willingness to give when the loved one is not able to reciprocate, whether it be because of illness, failure, or simply an hour of weakness. It is a love that can repair bonds severed by unfaithfulness, indifference, or jealousy."[3] The best example of this type of love is God Himself. "For God so loved the world that he *gave*" (John 3:16, emphasis added).

Many people who are happily married readily admit that they were attracted to their future husband or wife's personality and character long before they were fully aware of an appealing appearance. "I didn't notice he was such a nice-looking guy at first," is a comment you often hear from couples whose relationships have thrived upon many shared interests. Their physical attraction to one another was supported by a lasting foundation of friendship and respect.

REAL LOVE EDIFIES

We had known Jim and Leslie as single people for years and had seen their relationships with God develop and their personalities unfold. What we were amazed to observe, though, were the incredibly positive personality traits that surfaced in them as individuals as the result of their love for each other. Everyone who knew them well remarked on the differences. Leslie arrived places on time. Jim exhibited more sensitivity to people around him. And both were more self-confident and assured as individuals. No one should have been surprised, though, because real love produces positive, constructive changes in an individual.

But how many times have you heard comments like these: "I'm not surprised that Sandra forgot her dentist appointment today. She's in another world. Nothing else matters but spending time with Joe." We commonly expect someone "in love" to be irresponsible, living in a one-person world. That's the way they do it in movies and soap operas, after all! The idea is that when you're in love, your life centers around another person. "Joe is my reason for living." But when the fog clears and the reality dawns—if Joe is your reason for living, you haven't got much of a reason.

 When a couple is really in love, their relationship becomes a plus, not a replacement for other people and activities. Their love is secure enough to survive separation and mature enough to accept the responsibilities as well as the pleasures of the relationship.

Infatuated love, however, insists upon continual reassurance from the other person. It makes unreasonable demands that stem from possessiveness and insecurity.

Charted on graph paper, it would range from high peaks of certainty to valleys of doubt. Unstable in its duration, infatuation is like a seasonal monsoon; it comes, blows fiercely, and moves on.

ASK YOURSELF THESE QUESTIONS

As you consider whether what you're feeling is love, the kind that would prompt you to leave your present home and begin a new one, take careful stock of the quality of what you feel. Are you willing to wait for the fulfillment of that love as Jacob did? He "served seven years to get Rachel, but they seemed like only a few days to him because of his love for her" (Genesis 29:20).

Can you honestly say that you are willing to put that person's needs and desires ahead of your own? Is his or her happiness uppermost in your thinking? Hermann Oeser, a German author, writes, "Those who want to become happy should not marry. The important thing is to make the other one happy. Those who want to be understood should not marry. The important thing is to understand one's partner."[4]

Could your love thrive without physical expression? If your spouse had an accident that maimed or disfigured him or her for life, could you still care? Such are some of the questions and considerations you must weigh if you would accurately assess the quality of your love.

IS THERE ONLY ONE RIGHT PERSON?

One of Chuck Swindoll's great quips is that "success in life consists not so much in marrying the person who will make you happy as in escaping the many who could make you miserable."[5]

Most people who labor over the seriousness of a relationship struggle with the question, "Is there only one right person for me?" Many arduous, needle-in-a-haystack searches have taken place for the "right" partner. We would suggest that the question itself is a cul-de-sac.

After all, if it's true that we could only be happy with

one individual, then how does one explain the happy marriages in this world that are arranged by the parents? Or the individuals whose first wife or husband dies and when they remarry, they realize they have loved both individuals, only in different ways and at a different period of life?

It seems that God leads us along a journey in life in which our path crosses others. At a number of junctures, someone comes into our lives who might be considered a "suitable" match. Our labor is not in that perfectionistic search for "the right one" (which is really about the fear of failure). We need to invest our labor in making a spiritually wise choice.

Sometimes when we do premarital counseling we ask couples to list all the reasons why they would want to marry this particular individual. What we're looking for is whether there is some balance between the subjective part of relationship with the objective reality. Not just "how do I feel?" but "do I have an objective basis for this feeling?" In a good relationship, there will usually be a meshing of background, values, and personalities.

BACKGROUND

We each filter people around us through our background, almost subconsciously pursuing or rejecting relationships on the basis of racial, ethnic, socio-economic, and educational similarities or differences. (Although people who have opposite temperaments are often attracted to each other, social opposites seldom are.)

Only after marriage do most individuals really see how much their backgrounds come into play. They affect everything from how you celebrate holidays to whether you spend money on books or sirloin steaks. This is not to say that a high school graduate can never expect to be happily married to someone with a Ph.D., or that a marriage of a Korean and an American won't work. But it's better to face the differences squarely ahead of time.

It's true that in Christ "there is no Greek and Jew, circumcised or uncircumcised, barbarian, Scythian, slave or free" (Colossians 3:11). Yet it's also true that people with similar backgrounds have fewer points that rub against each other, and usually fewer adjustments.

VALUES

The values, goals, and outlook on life of two people in a relationship call for active, thoughtful discernment. Of course, the most fundamental value of them all is spiritual—how deeply is this individual committed to Christ?

Commitment to Christ comes in a variety of stripes and shapes. It's not enough to know that someone goes to church, or has "prayed the prayer," or was raised hearing Bible stories every night. Commitment is not based necessarily on how long someone has had a relationship with Jesus Christ—or how much they seem to know. The most significant factor is being confident that someone genuinely has a heart for God and a kind of open teachableness that enables them to respond to whatever God shows them.

Perhaps it would be helpful to picture the difference in a spiritual commitment by using these diagrams:

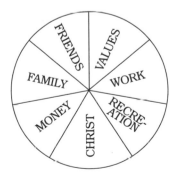 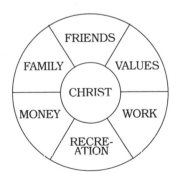

In the first, Christ is present but really, He is just one slice of the pie. An individual's relationship with the Lord Jesus is compartmentalized. Not much about it spills over into the rest of life. In the second illustration, Christ is more central and He has been given the free reign of all the rest. There is a conscious effort to allow His rightful rule of it all.

Sometimes two committed Christians who are strongly attracted to each other make the faulty assumption that "obviously, we should get married." Perhaps it is the first pure relationship they've had since they became Christians. But marriage is not always the next logical step to take. Often God brings a person into your life for the time being, without a lifetime relationship in mind. You have to give Him the freedom to do just that, without demanding more.

Going beyond the fundamental question of commitment to the Lord, consider how similar your goals and values are. Do you share a common mission in life, or is one person thinking about working with children in India, while the other prefers to stay within twenty miles of home? Does one of you envision a normal suburban lifestyle with well-groomed children and average church attendance, while the other really longs for something more radical and adventurous? How similar are the price tags you each place on people and relationships as opposed to material possessions?

Love that will work in marriage includes a fusing of the minds; you feel the same about the important things. You can bare your soul to the other person and be understood and accepted. You have conflicts and quarrels, but you can iron out your differences without devastating each other's sense of worth.

As you evaluate each other's tastes, preferences, and interests, how much do you have in common? If a basketball player marries an opera lover, their relationship will not automatically be doomed, but they will have to learn to enjoy, or at least endure, each other's interests. Otherwise sparks will fly and tension will be present. Do you share common interests . . . or are you at least honestly willing to move outside your comfort zone?

PERSONALITY

The last criterion for compatibility in relationships is explained in terms of *complementary* characteristics. We are attracted to people whose needs we can meet, and who in turn can meet some of our personality needs. Consciously or unconsciously, we enjoy the other's company because we experience a measure of completion in the presence of the other person.

There are lots of examples of this principle. George is a stable guy who thrives on being Sally's clear-headed, never-wavering partner. Sally in turn feels protected and secure with George. The person who is an impulsive, spur-of-the-moment planner is often attracted to someone who loves adventure. A talkative person usually enjoys a relationship with someone who is a good listener.

Complementary characteristics are not to be confused with *contradictory* needs that are sometimes used as examples when we say, "Opposites attract." The fact that Ann is punctual while Jim is inherently late, or that Jeff is a spendthrift and Janet is a tightwad, means that both partners in both marriages will have to compromise for the sake of maintaining peace.

Although no two people are completely compatible, and God does use your differences to build good things into each other's life, at some point you must face what those differences really are. Essentially, you must answer the question, How much do we have going for us and how much against us?

Whether or not you are seriously involved in a relationship with someone, take the opportunity to write down in as much detail as you want to, the character qualities and personality of the person you hope to marry someday. Pray about this list, and ask God to revise it as He desires. Then put it away somewhere. When you do begin to wonder if a particular relationship could develop into more than a friendship, compare the list to the person. Even though your needs and discernment may have changed with time, you will still find the list helpful. You can more quickly evaluate the relationship's potential.

WHEN YOU GET RIGHT DOWN TO IT

When you get right down to it, there are no formulas and no guarantees about choosing a life partner. It would be comforting, perhaps, if we could just fill out a questionnaire and allow a computer to match us with someone infinitely compatible. But relationships never fall into such neat categories.

The best advice that can be given is the simplest—wait and pray and seek the counsel of close friends. There's no way, though, to sanitize the uncertainty out of such a profound commitment to another human being. It's always a risk—but approached knowledgeably and in the fear of God, one well worth taking.

Ernest Boyer writes,

Although it is not always easy to recognize it as such, marriage is the most remarkable and most courageous of all human acts—the promise of two human beings to share life together on all levels, physical, economic, spiritual—a promise made in the face of certainty of death, the certainty of change, and the uncertainty of everything else. There is nothing else a human being might choose to do that is quite like this act, nothing so foolish or so profound.[6]

Once you've faced that squarely, you are probably ready to take a deep breath and embrace the "foolishness" of marriage as the wisest decision you will ever make.

Notes

1. James Peterson, as quoted in *Premarital Counseling* by Norman Wright (Chicago: Moody, 1977), p. 22.
2. Maxine Hancock, "Commitment That Endures," *Family Life Today*, March 1981, p. 20.
3. Robert K. Kelley, *Courtship, Marriage, and the Family* (New York: Harcourt Brace Jovanovich, 1974), p. 214.
4. Quoted by Walter Trobisch, *I Made You* (New York: Harper & Row, 1971), p. 75.
5. Charles R. Swindoll, *Singleness* (Portland, Oreg.: Multnomah, 1981), p. 13.
6. Ernest Boyer, *A Way in the World* (New York: Harper & Row, 1984), p. 75.

Questions for Personal Study and Application

1. How would you distinguish the difference in infatuation and love?
2. What are the characteristics of real love as listed in 1 Corinthians 13:4-7?
3. God's giving of His Son is the perfect example of real love. Read John 3:16 and Romans 5:8, and describe love as God practices it.
4. Read 2 Samuel 13:1-19.
   a. What evidence is there that Amnon was infatuated with Tamar?
   b. What were the results of Amnon's infatuation? (You might also read verses 23-38.)
5. What are some right and wrong reasons to marry?
6. Describe in as much detail as you wish the kind of person you hope to marry someday. Concentrate on his or her character qualities. Begin to pray regularly about your desires.
7. Waiting on God is essential in finding a mate. Look up Psalm 25:3, Isaiah 30:18 and 40:31, and Lamentations 3:25 and list the results of waiting and hoping in the Lord.
8. What personal application or commitment will result in your life, based on this study?

Suggested Scripture Memory

Matthew 6:33

Questions for Discussion

1. When you hear people speak of "love," what do you think they usually mean by that?

2. Look at 1 Corinthians 13. How can this passage be applied in evaluating a serious dating relationship?

4. When someone says, "I love you," what are some possible meanings attached to that phrase?

5. Is it possible that two people may love each other in a mature way and yet decide that marriage is not right for them? Can you give an example?

6. Do you believe there is only one right person for you to marry? Why, or why not?

7. How does Matthew 6:33 apply to looking for a mate or evaluating a serious dating relationship?

CHAPTER NINE

Growing into One
ා ා ා

Everyone fantasizes his personal version of that life-changing event—becoming engaged. Amid candlelight and roses, speaking with a hushed voice, the moment of truth arrives: "Will you marry me?" Only four simple words, and yet life is never the same because of them.

Somewhere en route to the altar, Stacy and I bypassed the candles and roses. But then, it helps if you understand that when Stacy makes up his mind to do something, he does it—right away. So after months of thinking and praying over the decision to marry, when he felt the time was right he wasted no time, walked into the nearest phone booth, and called me halfway across the country.

Imagine being awakened from a dead sleep to be asked, "Will you marry me?" Groggy and incoherent as I was, that was one time I was at no loss for words. Somehow, I was amazingly sure of my decision to marry Stacy.

For others, the circumstances vary, the question may be couched in different words, and the answer may be less confident; each situation is as unique as the two individuals taking part. Becoming engaged is the first step in the joining of two lives, the blending of two personalities, the potential of many generations to come.

Once you're engaged, allow enough time between the engagement and the wedding to give real thought to what it *means* to enter into marriage together. Most of us get lost in the details of planning for a wedding. And churches are chided, for becoming wedding factories—rather than specialists at helping people prepare for a lifelong union. The significant "work" to be done is really not lining up the best photographer in town—but learning the first real steps of what it feels like to walk in each other's shoes.

PREPARING FOR A LIFETIME TOGETHER

Getting married is the great merger of your life. Two strong personalities are getting ready to come together—and it's much better if you coalesce rather than collide. There are some principles which help that merger happen well.

BUILD A STRONG FOUNDATION

Years ago, the Air Force Academy in Colorado Springs embarked on a precedent-setting experiment. They chose a collection of their graduating cadets and offered a new thing called "premarital counseling" to engaged couples, hoping to see whether a good start in marriage added stability to the lives of young officers.

That experiment turned out to be such a bonanza—couples who had premarital counseling clearly did much better than those who did not—that the practice of offering help to a couple *before marriage* spread broadly. *Premarital counseling should be an integral part of any couple's wedding plans.* You may or may not have the resources to honeymoon in the Bahamas—but don't miss out on arranging individual sessions, if possible, with someone who is able to guide the process of premarital counseling. It's so much easier to help a couple get started well than to help them *undo* a tangled relationship ten years later.

After all, there's so much to talk about! This is the time to begin to develop your convictions together. Budgets, birth control, an expanded version of your life goals, how you want to raise children, what about your in-laws: every area of life takes on new meaning when there are two instead of one involved. It also helps to learn more about each others' "family-of-origin." How was anger handled in your family? What "roles" did your parents assume? Is there a significant loss or trauma in your past? The more you talk now, the fewer surprises you'll have on the other side of the altar.

We are sometimes asked how much a couple should share with each other about their past. Generally speaking, it's best to discuss anything from your past that might have an effect on your future relationship together. Trust is built on a foundation of honesty. If you have "secrets" from your past you are unable to reveal to the one closest to you, there will always be a nagging uncertainty about "whether he could really love me if he knew. . . ." If you love someone and God is leading you together, then your past—and his or her past—is all part of the package. Are there mistakes and failures there? Then you will both learn from them. Are there painful, shameful secrets? Then marriage is the place where you bind up each other's wounds with the same redemptive grace God has shown you.

Mike and Sarah met each other late in their twenties, each having experienced enough disappointment in relationships to really value the love they shared. Mike had made what felt like "huge sacrifices" to remain a virgin all those years. But Sarah had entered the faith only three years ago and her past was checkered with various men she'd known intimately. She'd made tremendous changes since she'd been a Christian. So many things were "right" about this relationship. But once engaged, the hurdle Mike had to cross was the pain of knowing that he would not be the first to share an intimate relationship with his wife and that pain surfaced all his old fears of inadequacy.

How does an engaged couple face such an impasse without it becoming this huge issue one or both trip over? A whole lot of talk and a great deal of prayer. The hard work of honesty and forgiveness and trusting God together is the only ground you can stand on that will give you solid footing. It can be done.

We're not suggesting that every last detail of the past has to be disclosed and agonized over. *But we are saying that secrets are the slow poison of relationships.* That's why "Speak the truth in love . . ." (Ephesians 4:15) is classic instruction on relationships within the body of Christ. When you face these issues before marriage, you invite a spirit of freedom, acceptance, and forgiveness that deepens your love. If the truth comes to light later it tends to poison your relationship with distrust and anger.

Engagement is the time when you also need to ask yourself if this person never changes—if he's just as quiet ten years from now, if she's just as disorganized—will you be willing to love them anyway? Don't marry with the idea of changing anyone but yourself. When each of us came to Christ, we said, in effect, "Lord, take me just as I am." We need to take each other in much the same way, just as we are. Marry someone you are willing to adjust to.

Engagement is the time to begin some of the good habits that will be "preventive maintenance" in your marriage. How will you, for instance, carve out quality time for each other? What will you do with conflict? Before we married (and then even more afterwards) we singled out one night a week where we went on a "date." We would go out for dinner or dessert, just to talk. It's amazing how much you can learn

about someone over a two-hour cup of coffee with no dis-
tractions. *Some of the simplest habits reap the biggest
dividends.* Continuing to "date" has been one of those for
us. And it all began during our engagement.

Another practice we happened on was the habit of keeping "short accounts." In other words, we were quick to ask
each other's forgiveness. Little things, big things, it didn't
matter. "I'm sorry, would you forgive me?" These were
words we just got accustomed to saying to each other. We
didn't let bad feelings stack up; we tried to keep the air
clear between us. When two strong people merge their lives
there's a lot of stepping on each other's toes in the daily
dance. And the word *apology* takes on new meaning.

Engagement is also the time to intensify the lifelong art
of studying your partner. What are her greatest needs? What
do his moods revolve around? How can we bring our conflicts to a point of mutual resolution? Marriage, as they say,
is an assault on selfishness. The focus has to change: how
does God intend to help me connect with this person in a
way that meets his deepest needs?

For a man to meet the deeper needs of his wife, he must
love her as Christ loved the Church in laying down his life for
her (Ephesians 5:25). An impossible feat apart from the grace
and power of God. A woman has a strong need for *security*
and a feeling of *worth and value*. She needs to know that
her husband is looking out for the family, that he's planning
in a certain direction. The cure for a nagging wife is a husband who becomes a planner and communicator.

Even in this day and age, when a woman's value is so
often measured by her standing in the marketplace, there
is no substitute for being valued in the eyes of her husband.
She longs to hear: "Tell me what you think about that idea,
honey." "I really need your opinion of this situation." Most
women value social intercourse (communication) as

intensely as their husbands value the sexual variety.

On the other hand, Scripture indicates that a man's greatest need is that of *respect*. "Wives, submit to your husbands as to the Lord. . . . The wife must respect her husband" (Ephesians 5:22,33). A man needs to feel that his wife is supporting him and willing to follow his leadership. A man might say, "Honey, I just need to feel the encouragement that you are on my team, that you're for me."

The needs of your partner may reveal themselves in many ways over the years, but they spring from the same roots. Engagement is the time to start developing your skill at assessing those needs.

Of all the things that you put on your wedding list, don't neglect prayer. Years later Stacy showed me a piece of paper where he'd written down things during our engagement that he began to pray for our relationship. It was amazing how God had answered those simple prayers—that our marriage would reflect Him, that he would be able to lead and provide well, that God would direct our paths, that we'd learn how to read each other well.

RESOLVE YOUR PAST CONFLICTS

If you admitted to a marriage counselor that you were $5,000 in debt, he'd advise you to take care of your debts, before considering marriage. It's just too much strain on a relationship to start out in the hole financially.

In the same way, emotional debts and broken relationships can become a strain on your marriage. Friction and conflict in especially intimate relationships such as with your mother or father, or your sister or brother, need to be mended, as much as possible, in order to emotionally leave home. It's part of that "leave and cleave" principle from Genesis 2:24 where in order to cleave well to each other, it's necessary to "leave" well what came before.

One friend related an interesting story about how she resolved her relationship with her brother before her marriage. "I realized there was an unspoken tension between us," she said, "mostly due to the rather overbearing way I treated him as my younger brother. I went to him and admitted my failures, asked his forgiveness, and started off on a new footing with him. It really helped to mend the fences between us. At least that's one rock I didn't carry into marriage."

Now is the time to deal with all your past debts, financial and otherwise. "If it is possible, as far as it depends on you, live at peace with everyone" (Romans 12:18).

YOU ARE, BUT THEN AGAIN YOU AREN'T

There is no time in your life like being an engaged couple. You aren't quite single any more, and goodness knows, you aren't married. Most of the time you are discussing life as it's going to be, not life as it is. You've waited with such anticipation to ask or answer the question, Will you marry me? Why, then, isn't engagement a state of perpetual ecstasy?

You will be comforted to know that for most people, engagement is a peculiar time of transition accompanied by predictable seasonal storms. For one thing, you are probably more tired than you realize. You may be weary of planning a wedding, tired of bouncing ideas back and forth between two sets of parents, and exhausted from finishing school or details at work. And while it is the event of a lifetime, the object of a wedding is to become husband and wife, not to stage the social event of the year. Many couples make the unfortunate mistake of beginning marriage so tired and exhausted that after the wedding they collapse on some remote beach.

Engagement has tremendous ups and downs. In your effort to be honest and transparent, don't make the mistake of sharing every negative emotion with your future spouse, unless you begin to have serious doubts about your prospective marriage. Just knowing that everyone goes through some of this should help. After all, you're making the second biggest decision of your life.

YOU'VE WAITED THIS LONG

Another tension most couples experience is in the physical arena. If you've waited this long to experience physical oneness, you can wait a few more months. It's terribly important that you do wait.

For one thing, you have to face the fact that 50 percent of the couples who say, "Let's get married," don't make it to the altar. Engagement is a time when either party can say, "I just don't think this is going to work." Sex only complicates the situation.

Secondly, you'll be far ahead in the challenge of sexual adjustment if you enter marriage free from guilt. One pastor we know asks each couple he marries to write out a contract together of the limits they will set in physical involvement during their engagement period. Then he says, "Mark it down that I am personally going to ask you on the day that I marry you if you kept this agreement. I want you to be able to look your children straight in the eye when you tell them *why* they must be home by midnight."

Maybe you won't go as far as signing a piece of paper, but you must discuss the limits of your involvement. The temptation to proceed on to the point of no return is incredible.

THE RIGHT PERSON AT THE RIGHT TIME

There's more to getting married than finding "the right person." To ensure the smoothest transition from single to married life, you will want to marry at the right time. What is the best length for an engagement period? Perhaps you've known couples who were engaged three weeks, and others, three years. Today they're happily married.

Generally speaking, the engagement period needs to be long enough to confirm or negate your decision to marry, and short enough to keep from losing your mind. William Coleman aptly states, "The engagement period is not the best time to get to know each other. Date each other for one, two, three, ten years if you want. But once you say, 'We are going to get married,' do not pass Go and do not collect $200. Take the shortest route to the altar and get married. If you are not prepared to get married for a year or more, don't get engaged."[1]

Obviously there are extenuating circumstances. Weddings must be paid for; you'd like your families to be well and present; it would be wise to have a job. But the principle remains: If you have to wait much longer than a year, then wait to get engaged.

As you consider the question, When should we get married? be careful how many *new* things you will tackle at one time. Three days after we got married, we moved halfway across the country to a town new to us both, where we knew no one, to a new job, and to a new relationship—ours. It took us a few months to realize that most people don't do this and that we'd taken on too many new things at once.

Anticipate and plan your wedding together as much as possible, especially the ceremony. Enjoy working together on a common project. But try hard not to get lost in the details or end up debating your future sister-in-law over the merits of stainless steel. The object is to get married with your friendships intact and your relations still speaking to each other!

CHRISTIAN MARRIAGE—A LIFETIME COMMITMENT

A friend of ours who married at a very young age once told me that on her honeymoon she began to feel she'd made a terrible mistake. She called her father in tears and told him she wanted to come home and forget the whole thing. "Honey," he said, "those vows you made the other day, you made before God. And He is the one who will help you work them out. You stay right where you are." She took her father's advice, and twenty-five years later she's very glad she did.

Most of us never reach such an extremity, especially on our honeymoon. But it's good to remember that the vows you take before friends and family, you also repeat before the living God. Those words cannot be spoken lightly. C. S. Lewis said we sign a contract when we marry because we realize that there will be periods of conflict, boredom, and monotony. We know ahead of time that we will "fall out of love" with our spouse, in that breathless sense, and marriage is what keeps us in place until we learn the durable variety of love that comes later.

Marriage can take you to some of the greatest heights you've ever known. Then again, there are days when you wonder how two such different people ever got together. I love to reread a statement that Dick Halverson made about his own marriage.

> The first element is commitment, despite the differences. My wife and I are married for life. I have an arrangement with Doris that God witnessed as an unconditional covenant for life. No matter how difficult it is to live together, we are going to stay married. Every struggle we have that could be used as an excuse to separate or divorce is the very material

God wants us to use to create intimacy in our marriage. We can't get it any other way; it comes by hammer and heat. Good marriages are always forged.[2]

Early on in our marriage, after one of those clashing disagreements, Stacy said, "Honey, you know that I'm just a sinner, shot through and through." I nicknamed him the "big sinner," and the name has stuck through the years. He calls me the "little sinner" (no reference to the quantity of sin intended). Even now we occasionally refer to each other by our nicknames (especially during times of stress) because those names remind us that we're just two sinners married to each other.

Marriage is a private school in which you can develop the love that says, "I accept you even if I have to listen to the same corny jokes for the next fifty years." As two people learn the real meaning of love, hashing through the daily realities of life together, they emerge better equipped to love others outside of their classroom.

Charlie Shedd has been known for his illustrations about marriage. He likens the merging of two people into one entity to two streams that converge at one point with great force, even considerable spray and foam. But eventually, from their union a river emerges, luxuriously broad and deep.

Marriage is an adventure that begins at an altar and ends at a graveside. In between there will be laughter and tears, anger and ecstasy. As the Lord brought you together, He will see you through. May you always turn back to Him, who was and who is and who is to come, for "unless the LORD builds the house, its builders labor in vain" (Psalm 127:1).

Notes
1. William L. Coleman, *Engaged* (Wheaton, Ill.: Tyndale, 1980), p. 23.
2. "Planting Seeds and Watching Them Grow," an interview with Dr. Richard C. Halverson, *Leadership*, Fall 1980, p. 19.

142 Growing into One

Questions for Personal Study and Application

1. Do you believe that marriage has some guarantees; for example, that you will never have to make another decision by yourself? If so, what are these guarantees?
2. What do you believe are the purposes of engagement?
3. What are some topics and questions an engaged couple needs to talk about?
4. What are some ways in which Satan might attempt to damage or destroy a strong Christian relationship between an engaged couple?
5. While they were engaged, the authors began two important practices to strengthen their marriage. What did they do? What are some things you think might be important habits to form as a couple?
6. To what degree do you "marry" your in-laws? Should your attitude and relationship with them be a consideration in getting married?

Suggested Scripture Memory

Psalm 127:1

Questions for Discussion

2. Are there any topics about which a difference of opinion is important enough to indicate that a couple should not get married? If so, what do you think they are?
3. How much time, in general, do you think it takes to plan the wedding and make other arrangements, such as a place to live?
4. How would you go about setting guidelines for your physical relationship?

5. If an engaged couple disagrees about some decisions concerning the wedding, how should they be handled?
6. What are some requests you would include as you regularly prayed about your approaching marriage?
7. What can you do to make engagement a joyful time, not just a busy time?
8. How important is it to speak to the parents of the girl before you propose formally?

Authors

ᴑ ᴑ ᴐ

STACY T. RINEHART

Stacy T. Rinehart, ThM., D Min. serves as the International Director for MentorLink (www.MentorLink.org). Stacy is author of *Upside Down: The Paradox of Servant Leadership* (NavPress). Stacy has thirty years experience developing leaders internationally, cross-culturally, and cross-organizationally.

He served as Executive Director of Training and Materials for The CoMission, a consortium of eighty-four mission agencies, which in the 1990s trained and placed 205 teams of internationals in sixty-eight cities of the former Soviet Union to minister among public school teachers.

He served as a Vice President for the Navigators overseeing the US Cities ministries and later representing the Navigators in the Body of Christ in formal partnerships.

Stacy and his wife Paula have been married for twenty-nine years and have two grown children.

PAULA RINEHART

Paula Rinehart, MSW, is a marriage and family counselor, a women's conference speaker, and the author of *Strong Women, Soft Hearts* (W Publishing). She served for a number of years with her husband, Stacy, on the staff of The Navigators. The Rineharts live in Raleigh, North Carolina. They have two grown children.